THE TRAIL OF THE WHITE MULE

by

B. M. Bower

CHAPTER ONE

Casey Ryan, hunched behind the wheel of a large, dark blue touring car with a kinked front fender and the glass gone from the left headlight, slid out from the halted traffic, shied sharply away from a hysterically clanging street car, crossed the path of a huge red truck coming in from his right, missed it with two inches to spare and was halfway down the block before the traffic officer overtook him.

The traffic officer was Irish too, and bigger than Casey, and madder. For all that, Casey offered to lick the livin' tar outa him before accepting a pale, expensive ticket which he crumbled and put into his pocket without looking at it.

"What I know about these here fancy city rules ain't sufficient to give a horntoad a headache—but it's a darn sight more'n I care," Casey declaimed hotly. "I never was asked what I thought of them tin signs you stick up on the end of a telegraft pole, to tell folks when to go an' when to quit goin'. Mebby it's all right fer these here city drivers—"

"This'll mean thirty days for you," spluttered the officer. "I ought to call the patrol right now—"

"Get the undertaker on the line first!" Casey advised him ominously.

Traffic was piling up behind them, and horns were honking a blatant chorus that extended two blocks up the street. The traffic officer glanced into the troubled gray eyes of the Little Woman beside Casey and took his foot off the running board.

"Better go put up your bail and then forfeit it," he advised in a milder tone. "The judge will probably remember you; I do, and my memory ain't the best in the world. Twice you've been hooked for speeding through traffic; and parking by fire-plugs and in front of the No Park signs and after four, seems to be your big outdoor sport. Forfeit your bail, old boy—or it's thirty days for you, sure."

Casey Ryan made bitter retort, but the traffic cop had gone to untangle two furious Fords from a horse-drawn mail wagon, so he did not hear. Which was good luck for Casey.

"Why do you persist in making trouble for yourself?" the Little Woman beside him exclaimed. "It can't be so hard to obey the rules; other drivers do. I know that I have driven this car all over town without any trouble whatever."

Casey hogged the next safety-zone line to the deep disgust of a young movie star in a cream-and-silver racer, and pulled in to the curb just where he could not be passed.

"All right, ma'am. You can drive, then." He slid out of the driver's seat to the pavement, his face a deeper shade of red than usual.

"For pity's sake, Casey! Don't be silly," his wife cried sharply, a bit of panic in her voice.

"You was in a hurry to git home," Casey pointed out to her with that mildness of manner which is not mild. "I was hurryin', wasn't I?"

"You aren't hurrying now—you're delaying the traffic again. Do be reasonable! You know it costs money to argue with the police."

"Police be damned! I'm tryin' to please a woman, an' I'm up agin a hard proposition. You can ask anybody if I'm the unreasonable one. You hustled me out of the show soon as the huggin' commenced. You wouldn't even let me stay to see the first of Mutt and Jeff. You said you was in a hurry. I leaves the show without seein' the best part, gits the car an' drills through the traffic tryin' to git yuh home quick. Now you're kickin' because I did hurry."

"Hey! Whadda yuh mean, blockin' the traffic?" a domineering voice behind him bellowed. "This ain't any reception hall, and it ain't no free auto park neither."

Another traffic officer with another pencil and another pad of tickets such as drivers dread to see began to write down the number of Casey's car. This man did not argue. He finished his work briskly, presented another notice which advised Casey Ryan to report immediately to police headquarters, waved Casey peremptorily to proceed, and returned to his little square platform to the chorus of blatting automobile horns.

"The cops in this town hands out tickets like they was Free Excursion peddlers!" snorted Casey, his eyes a pale glitter behind his half-closed lids. "They can go around me, or they can honk and be darned to 'em. Git behind the wheel, ma'am—Casey Ryan's drove the last inch he'll ever drive in this darned town. If they pinch me again, it'll have to be fer walkin'."

The Little Woman looked at him, pressed her lips together and moved behind the wheel. She did not say a word all the way out to the white apartment house on Vermont which held the four rooms they called home. She parked the car dexterously in front and led the way to their apartment (ground floor, front) before she looked at me.

"It's coming to a show-down, Jack," she said then with a faint smile. "He's on probation already for disobeying traffic rules of one sort and other, and his fines cost more than the entire upkeep of the car. I think he really will have to go to jail this time. It just isn't in Casey Ryan to take orders from any one, especially when his own personal habits of driving a car are concerned."

"Town life is getting on his nerves," I tried to defend Casey, and at the same time to comfort the Little Woman. "I didn't think it would work, his coming here to live, with nothing to do but spend money. This is the inevitable result of too much money and too much leisure."

"It sounds much better, putting it that way," murmured Mrs. Casey. "I think you're right—though he did behave back there as if it were too much matrimony. Jack, he's been looking forward to your visit. I'm sorry this has happened to spoil it."

"It isn't spoiled," I grinned. "Casey Ryan is, always and ever shall be Casey Ryan. He's running true to form, though tamer than one would expect. When do you think he'll show up?"

Mrs. Casey did not know. She ventured a guess or two, but there was no conviction in her tone. With two nominal arrests in five minutes chalked against him, and with his first rebellion against the Little Woman to rankle in his conscience and memory, she owned herself at a loss.

With a cheerfulness that was only conversation deep, we waited for Casey and finally ate supper without him. The evening was enlivened somewhat by Babe's chatter of kindergarten doings; and was punctuated by certain pauses while steps on the sidewalk passed on or ended with the closing of another door than the Ryans'. I fought the impulse to call up the police station, and I caught the eyes of the Little Woman straying unconsciously to the telephone in the hall while she talked of things remote from our inner thoughts. Margaret Ryan is game, I'll say that. We played cribbage for an hour or two, and the Little Woman beat me until finally I threw up my hands and quit.

"I can't stand it any longer, Mrs. Casey. Do you think he's in jail, or just sulking at a movie somewhere?" I blurted. "Forgive my butting in, but I wish you'd talk about it. You know you can, to me. Casey Ryan is a friend and more than a friend: he's a pet theory of mine—a fad, if you prefer to call him that.

"I consider him a perfect example of human nature in its unhampered, unbiased state, going straight through life without deviating a hair's breadth from the viewpoint of youth. A fighter and a castle builder; a sort of rough-edged Peter Pan. Till he gums soft food and hobbles with a stick because the years have warped his back and his legs, Casey Ryan will keep that indefinable, bubbling optimism of spiritual youth. So tell me all about him. I want to know who has licked, so far; luxury or Casey Ryan."

The Little Woman laughed and picked up the cards, evening their edges with sensitive fingers that had not been manicured so beautifully when first I saw them.

"Well-sir," she drawled, making one word of the two and failing to keep a little twitching from her lips, "I think it's been about a tie, so far. As a husband —Casey's a darned good bachelor." Her chuckle robbed that statement of anything approaching criticism. "Aside from his insisting on cooking breakfast every morning and feeding me in bed, forcing me to eat fried eggs and sour-dough hotcakes swimming in butter and honey—when I crave grapefruit and thin toast and one French lamb chop with a white paper frill on the handle and garnished with fresh parsley—he's the soul of consideration. He wants four kinds of jam on the table every meal, when fresh fruit is going to waste. He's bullied the laundryman until the poor fellow's reached the point where he won't stop if the car's parked in front and Casey's liable to be home; but aside from that, Casey's all right.

"After serving time in the desert and rustling my own wood and living on bacon and beans and sour-dough bread, I'm perfectly willing to spend the rest of my life doing painless housekeeping with all the modern built-in features ever invented; and buying my bread and cakes and salads from the delicatessen around the corner. I never want to see a sagebush again as long as I live, or feel the crunch of gravel under my feet. I expect to die in French-heeled pumps and embroidered silk stockings and the finest, silliest silk things ever put in a show window to tempt the soul of a woman. But it took just two weeks and three days to drive Casey back to his sour-dough can."

"He craved luxury more than you seemed to do," I remembered aloud.

"He did, yes. But his idea of luxury is sitting down in the kitchen to a real meal of beans and biscuits and all the known varieties of jam and those horrible whitewashed store cookies and having the noise of the phonograph drowned every five minutes by a passing street car. Casey wants four movies a day, and he wants them all funny. He brings home silk shirts with the stripes fairly shrieking when he unwraps them—and he has to be thrown and tied to get a collar on him.

"He will get up at any hour of the night to chase after a fire engine, and every whipstitch he gets pinched for doing something which is perfectly lawful and right in the desert and perfectly awful in the city. You saw him," said the Little Woman, "to-day." And she added wistfully, "It's the first time since we were married that he has ever talked back—to me.

"And you know," she went on, shuffling the cards and stopping to regard the joker attentively (though I am sure she didn't know what card she was looking at), "just chasing around town and doing nothing but square yourself for not playing according to the rules costs money without getting you anywhere. Fifty-five thousand dollars isn't so much just to play with, in this town. Casey's highest ambition now seems to be nickel disk wheels on a new racing car that can make the speed cops go some to catch him. His idea of economy is to put six or seven thousand dollars into a car that will enable him to outrun a twenty-dollar fine!

"We have some money invested," she went on. "We own this apartment house —and fortunately it's in my name. So long as the housing problem continues critical, I think I can keep Casey going without spending our last cent."

"He did one good stroke of business," I ventured, "when he bought this place. Apartment houses are good as gold mines these days."

The Little Woman laughed. "Well-sir, it wasn't so much a stroke as it was a wallop. Casey bought it just to show who was boss, he or the landlord. The first thing he did when we moved in was to take down the nicely framed rules that said we must not cook cabbage nor onions nor fish, nor play music after ten o'clock at night, nor do any loud talking in the halls.

"Every day for a week Casey cooked cabbage, onions and fish. He sat up nights to play the graphophone. He stayed home to talk loudly and play bucking bronk with Babe all up and down the stairs and in the halls. Our rent was paid for a month in advance, and the landlord was too little and old to fight. So he sold out cheap—and it really was a good stroke of business for us, though not deliberate.

"Well-sir, at first we lost tenants who didn't enjoy the freedom of their neighbors' homes. But really, Jack, you'd be surprised to know how many people in this city just LOVE cabbage and onions and fish, and to have children they needn't disown whenever they go house-hunting. I had ventilator hoods put over every gas range in the house, and turned the back yard into a playground with plenty of sand piles and swings. I raised the price, too, and made the place look very select, with a roof garden for the grown-ups. We have the house filled now with really nice families—avoiding the garlic brand —and as an investment I wouldn't ask for anything better.

"Casey enjoyed himself hugely while he was whipping things into shape, but the last month he's been going stale. The tenants are all so thankful to do as they please that they're excruciatingly polite to him, no matter what he does or says. He's tired of the beaches and he has begun to cuss the long, smooth roads that are signed so that he couldn't get lost if he tried. It does seem as if there's no interest left in anything, unless he can get a kick out of going to jail. And, Jack, I do believe he's gone there."

The telephone rang and the Little Woman excused herself and went into the hall, closing the door softly behind her.

I'm not greatly given to reminiscence, but while I sat and watched the flames of civilization licking tamely at the impregnable iron bark of the gas logs, the eyes of my memory looked upon a picture:

Desert, empty and with the mountains standing back against the sky, the great dipper uptilted over a peak and the stars bending close for very friendliness. The licking flames of dry greasewood burning, with a pungent odor in my nostrils when the wind blew the smoke my way. The far-off hooting of an owl, perched somewhere on a juniper branch watching for mice; and Casey Ryan sitting cross-legged in the sand, squinting humorously at me across the fire while he talked.

I saw him, too, bolting a hurried breakfast under a mesquite tree in the chill before sunrise, his mind intent upon the trail; facing the desert and its hardships as a matter of course, with never a thought that other men would shrink from the ordeal.

I saw him kneeling before a solid face of rock in a shallow cut in the hillside, swinging his "single-jack" with tireless rhythm; a tap and a turn of the steel, a tap and a turn—chewing tobacco industriously and stopping now and then to pry off a fresh bit from the plug in his hip pocket before he reached for the "spoon" to muck out the hole he was drilling.

I saw him larruping in his Ford along a sandy, winding trail it would break a snake's back to follow, hot on the heels of his next adventure, dreaming of the fortune that finally came. . . .

The Little Woman came in looking as if she had been talking with Destiny and was still dazed and unsteady from the meeting.

"Well-sir, he's gone!" she announced, and stopped and tried to smile. But her eyes looked hurt and sorry. "He has bought a Ford and a tent and outfit since he left us down on Seventh and Broadway, and he just called me up on long-distance from San Bernardino. He's going out on a prospecting trip, he says. I'll say he's been going some! A speed cop overhauled him just the other side of Claremont, he told me, and he was delayed for a few minutes while he licked the cop and kicked him and his motorcycle into a ditch. He says he's sorry he sassed me, and if I can drive a car in this darned town and not spend all my loose change paying fines, I'm a better man than he is. He doesn't know when he'll be back—and there you are."

She sat down wearily on the arm of an over-stuffed armchair and looked up at the gilt-and-onyx clock which I suspected Casey of having bought. "If he isn't lynched before morning," she sighed whimsically, "he'll probably make it to the Nevada line all right."

I rose, also glancing at the clock. But the Little Woman put up a hand to forbid the plan she read in my mind.

"Let him alone, Jack," she advised. "Let him go and be just as wild and devilish as he wants to be. I'm only thankful he can take it out on a Ford and a pick and shovel. There really isn't any trouble between us two. Casey knows I can look out for myself for awhile. He's got to have a vacation from loafing and matrimony. I'm so thankful he isn't taking it in jail!"

I told her somewhat bluntly that she was a brick, and that if I could get in touch with Casey I'd try to keep an eye on him. It would probably be a good thing, I told her, if he did stay away long enough to let this collection of complaints against him be forgotten at the police station.

I went away, hoping fervently that Casey would break even his own records that night. I really intended to find him and keep an eye on him. But keeping an eye on Casey Ryan is a more complicated affair than it sounds.

Wherefore, much of this story must be built upon my knowledge of Casey and a more or less complete report of events in which I took no part, welded together with a bit of healthy imagination.

CHAPTER TWO

Casey Ryan knew his desert. Also, from long and not so happy experience, he knew Fords, or thought he did. He made the mistake, however, of buying a nearly new one and asking it to accomplish the work of a twin six from the moment he got behind the wheel.

He was fortunate in buying a demonstrator's car with a hundred miles or so to its credit. He arrived in Barstow before the proprietor of a supply store had gone to bed—for which he was grateful to the Ford. He loaded up there with such necessities for desert prospecting as he had not waited to buy in Los Angeles, turned short off the main highway where traffic officers might be summoned by telephone to lie in wait for him, and took the steeper and less used trail north. He was still mad and talking bitterly to himself in an undertone while he drove—telling the new Ford what he thought of city rules and city ways, and driving it as no Ford was ever meant by its maker to be driven.

The country north of Barstow is not to be taken casually in the middle of a dark night, even by Casey Ryan and a Ford. The roads, once you are well away from help, are all pretty much alike, and all bad. And although the white, diamond-shaped signs of a beneficent automobile club are posted here and there, where wrong turnings are most likely to prove disastrous to travelers, Casey Ryan was in the mood to lick any man who pointed out a sign to him. He did see one or two in spite of himself and gave a grunt of contempt. So, where he should have turned to the east (his intention being to reach Nevada by way of Silver Lake) he continued traveling north and didn't know it.

Driving across the desert on a dark night is confusing to the most observant wayfarer. On either side, beyond the light of the car, illusory forest stands for mile upon mile. Up hill or down or across the level it is the same—a narrow, winding trail through dimly seen woods. The most familiar road grows strange; the miles are longer; you drive through mystery and silence and the world around you is a formless void.

Dawn and a gorgeous sunrise painted out the woods and revealed barren hilltops which Casey did not know. Because he did not know them, he guessed shrewdly that he was on his way to the wilderness of mountains and sand which lies west of Death Valley. Small chance he had of hearing the shop whistles blow in Las Vegas at noon, as he had expected.

He was telling himself that he didn't care where he went, when the car, laboring more and more reluctantly up a long, sandy hill, suddenly stopped. In Casey's heart was a thrill at the sheer luxury of stopping in the middle of the road without having some thick-necked cop stride toward him bawling insults. That he was obliged to stop, and that a hill uptilted before him, and the sand was a foot deep outside the ruts failed to impress him with foreboding. He gloried in his freedom and thought not at all of the Ford.

He climbed stiffly out, squinted at the sky line, which was jagged, and at his immediate surroundings, which were barren and lonely and soothing to his soul that hungered for these things. Great, gaunt "Joshua" trees stood in grotesque groups all up and down the narrow valley, hiding the way he had come from the way he would go. It was as if the desert had purposely dropped a curtain before his past and would show him none of his future. Whereat Casey Ryan grinned, took a chew of tobacco and was himself again.

"If they wanta come pinch me here, I'll meet 'em man to man. Back in town no man's got a show. They pile in four deep and gang a feller. Out here it's lick er git licked. They can all go t' thunder. Tahell with town!"

The odor of coffee boiling in a new pot which the sagebrush fire was fast blackening; the salty, smoky smell of bacon frying in a new frying pan that turned bluish with the heat; the sizzle of bannock batter poured into hot grease —these things made the smiling mouth of Casey Ryan water with desire.

"Hell!" said Casey, breathing deep when, stomach full and resentment toward the past blurred by satisfaction with his present, he filled his pipe and fingered his vest pocket for a match. "Gas stoves can't cook nothin' so there's any taste to it. That there's the first real meal I've et in six months. Light a match and turn on the gas and call that a fire! Hunh! Good old sage er greasewood fer Casey Ryan, from here on!"

He laid back against the sandy sidehill, tilted his hat over his eyes and crossed his legs luxuriously. He was in no hurry to continue his journey. Now that he and the desert were alone together, haste and Casey Ryan held nothing in common. For awhile he watched a Joshua palm that looked oddly like a giant man with one arm hanging loose at its side and another pointing fixedly at a distant, black-capped butte standing aloof from its fellows. Casey was tired after his night on the trail. Easy living in town had softened his muscles and slowed a little that untiring energy which had balked at no hardship. He was drowsy, and his brain stopped thinking logically and slipped into half-waking fancy.

The Joshua seemed to move, to lift its arm and point more imperatively toward the peak. Its ungainly head seemed to turn and nod at Casey. What did the darned thing want? Casey would go when he, got good and ready. Perhaps he would go that way, and perhaps he would not. Right here was good enough for Casey Ryan at present; and you could ask anybody if he were the man to follow another man's pointing, much less a Joshua tree.

Battering rain woke Casey some hours later and drove him to the shelter of the Ford. Thunder and lightning came with the rain, and a bellowing wind that rocked the car and threatened once or twice to overturn it. With some trouble Casey managed to button down the curtains and sat huddled on the front seat, watching through a streaming windshield the buffeted wilderness. He was glad he had not unloaded his outfit; gladder still that the storm had not struck which he was traveling. Down the trail toward him a small river galloped, washing deep gullies where the wheels of his car offered obstruction to its boisterousness.

"She's a tough one," grinned Casey, in spite of the chattering of his teeth. "Looks like all the water in the world is bein' poured down this pass. Keeps on, I'll have to gouge out a couple of Joshuays an' turn the old Ford into a boat —but Casey'll keep agoin'!"

Until inky dark it rained like the deluge. Casey remained perched in his one-man ark and tried hard to enjoy himself and his hard-won freedom. He stabbed open a can of condensed milk, poured it into a cup, and drank it and ate what was left of his breakfast bannock, which he had fortunately put away in the car out of the reach of a hill of industrious red ants.

He thought vaguely of cranking the car and going on, but gave up the notion. One sidehill, he decided, was as good as another sidehill for the present.

That night Casey slept fitfully in the car and discovered that even a wall bed in a despised apartment house may be more comfortable than the front seat of a Ford. His bones ached by morning, and he was hungry enough to eat raw bacon and relish it. But the sun was fighting through the piled clouds and shone cheerfully upon the draggled pass, and Casey boiled coffee and fried bacon and bannock beside the trail, and for a little while was happy again.

From breakfast until noon he was busy as a beaver repairing the washout beneath the car and on to the top of the hill. She was going to have to get down and dig in her toes to make it, he told the Ford, when at last he heaved pick and shovel into the tonneau, packed in his cooking outfit and made ready to crank up.

From then until supper time he wore a trail around the car, looking to see what was wrong and why he could not crank. He removed hootin'-annies and dingbats (using Casey's mechanical terms) looked them over dissatisfiedly, and put them back without having done them ny good whatever. Sometimes they were returned to a different place, I imagine, since I know too well how impartial Casey is with the mechanical parts of a Ford.

He made camp there that night, pitching his little tent in the trail for pure cussedness, and defying aloud a traveling world to make him move until he got good and ready. He might have saved his vocabulary, for the road was impassable before him and behind; and had Casey managed to start the car, he could not have driven a mile in either direction.

Since he did not know that, the next day he painstakingly cleaned the spark plugs and tried again to crank the Ford; couldn't, and removed more hootin'-annies and dingbats than he had touched the day before. That night he once more pitched his tent in the trail, hoping in his heart that some one would drive along and dispute his right to camp there; when he would lick the doggone cuss.

On the fourth day, after a long, fatiguing session with the vitals of a Ford that refused to be cranked, Casey was busy gathering brush, for his supper fire when Fate came walking up' the trail. Fate appears in many forms. In this instance it assumed the shape of a packed burro that poked its nose around a group of Joshuas, stopped abruptly and backed precipitately into another burro which swung out of the trail and went careening awkwardly down the slope. The stampeding burro had not seen the Ford at all, but accepted the testimony of its leader that something was radically wrong with the trail ahead. His pack bumped against the yuccas as he went; after him lurched a large man, heavy to the point of fatness, yelling hoarse threats and incoherent objurgations.

Casey threw down his armful of dead brush and went after the lead burro which was blazing itself a trail in an entirely different direction. The lead burro had four large canteens strapped outside its pack, and Casey was growing so short of water that he had begun to debate seriously the question of draining the radiator on the morrow.

I don't suppose many of you would believe the innate cussedness of a burro when it wants to be that way. Casey hazed this one to the hills and back down the trail for half a mile before he rushed it into a clump of greasewood and sneaked up on it when it thought itself hidden from all mortal eyes. After that he dug heels into the sand and hung on. Memory resurrected for his need certain choice phrases coined in times of stress for the ears of burros alone. Luxury and civilization and fifty-five thousand dollars and a wife were as if they had never been. He was Casey Ryan, the prospector, fighting a stubborn donkey all over a desert slope. He led it conquered back to the Ford, tied it to a wheel and lifted off the four canteens, gratified with their weight and hoping there were more on the other burro. He had quite forgotten that he had meant to lick the first man he saw, and grinned when the fat man came toiling back with the other animal.

By the time their coffee was boiled and their bacon fried, each one knew the other's past history and tentative plans for the future, censored and glossed somewhat by the teller but received without question or criticism.

The fat man's name was Barney Oakes, and he had heard of Casey Ryan and was glad to meet him. Though Casey had never heard of Barney Oakes, he discovered that they both knew Bill Masters, the garage man at Lund; and further gossip revealed the amazing fact that Barney Oakes had once been the husband of the woman whom Casey had very nearly married, the widow who cooked for the Lucky Lode.

"Boy, you're sure lucky she turned loose on yuh before yuh went an' married her!" Barney congratulated Casey, slapping his great thigh and laughing loudly. "She shore is handy with her tongue—that old girl. Ever hear a sawmill workin' overtime? That's her—rippin' through knots an' never blowin' the whistle fer quittin' time. I never knowed a man could have as many faults as what she used t' name over fer me." He drained his cup and sighed with great content. "At that, I stayed with her seven months and fourteen days," he boasted. "I admit, two of them months I was laid up with a busted ankle an' shoulder blade. Tunnel caved in on me."

They talked late that night and were comrades, brothers, partners share and share alike before they slept. Next morning Casey tried again to start the Ford; couldn't; and yielded to Barney's argument that burros were better than a car for prospectin' in that rough country. They overhauled Casey's outfit, took all the grub and as much else as the burros could carry and debated seriously what point in the Panamints they should aim for.

"Where's that there Joshuay tree pointin' to?" Casey asked finally. "She's the biggest and oldest in the bunch, and ever since I've been here she's looked like she's got somethin' on 'er mind. Whadda yuh think, Barney?"

Barney walked around the yucca, stood behind the extended arm, squinted at the sharp-peaked butte with the black capping, toward which the gaunt tree seemed to point. He spat out a stale quid of tobacco and took a fresh one, squinted again toward the butte and looked at Casey.

"She's country I never prospected in, back in there. I've follered poorer advice than a Joshuay. Le's try it a whirl."

Thus it came to pass that Casey Ryan forsook his Ford for a strange partner with two burros and a clouded past, and fared forth across the barren foothills with no better guidance than the rigid, outstretched limb of a great, gaunt Joshua tree.

CHAPTER THREE

In a still sunny gulch which shadows would presently fill to the brim, Casey Ryan was reaching, soiled bandanna in his hand, to pull a pot of bubbling coffee from the coals,—a pot now blackened with the smoke of many campfires to prove how thoroughly a part of the open land it had become. Something nipped at his right shoulder, and at the same instant ticked the coffeepot and overturned it into a splutter of steam and hot ashes. The spiteful crack of a rifle shot followed close. Casey ducked behind a nose of rock, and big Barney Oakes scuttled for cover, spilling bacon out of the frying pan as he went.

For a week the two had been camped in this particular gulch, which drew in to a mere wrinkle on the southwestern slope of the black-topped butte, toward which the Joshua tree in the pass had directed them. Nearly a week they had spent toiling across the hilly, waterless waste, with two harrowing days when their canteens flopped empty on the burros and big Barney stumbled oftener than Casey liked to see. Casey himself had gone doggedly ahead, his body bent forward, his square shoulders sagging a bit, but with never a thought of doing anything but go on.

A red splotch high up on the side of this gulch promised "water formation" as prospectors have a way of putting it. They had found the water, else adventure would have turned to tragedy. Near the water they had also found a promising outcropping of silver-bearing quartz. Barney's blowpipe had this very day shown them silver in castle-building quantities.

Just at this moment, however, they were not thinking of mines. They were eyeing a round hole in the coffeepot from which a brown rivulet ran spitting into the blackening coals.

Casey was the more venturesome. He raised himself to see if he could discover where the bullet had come from, and very nearly met the fate of the coffeepot. He felt the wind of a second bullet that spatted against a boulder near Barney. Barney burrowed deeper into his covert.

Casey went down on all fours and crawled laboriously toward a concealing bank covered thick with brush. A third bullet clipped a twig of sage just about three inches above the middle of his back, and Casey flattened on his stomach and swore. Some one on the peak of the hill had good eyesight, he decided. Neither spoke, other than to swear in undertones; for voices carried far in that clear atmosphere, and nothing could be gained by conversation.

Darkness never had poured so slowly into that gulch since the world was young. The campfire had died to black embers before Casey ventured from his covert, and Barney Oakes seemed to have holed up for the season. Unless you have lived for a long while in a land altogether empty of any human life save your own, you cannot realize the effect of having mysterious bullets zip past your ears and ruin your supper for you.

"Somebody's gunnin' fer us, looks like t' me," Barney observed belatedly in a hoarse whisper, from his covert.

"Found that out, did yuh? Well, it ain't the first time Casey's been shot at and missed," Casey retorted peevishly in the lee of the bank. "Say! I knowed the sing of bullets before I was old enough to carry a tune."

"So'd I," boasted Barney, "but that ain't sayin' I learned t' like the song."

"What I'm figurin' out now," said Casey, "is how to get up there an' AT 'am. An' how we kin do it without him seein' us. Goin' t' be kinda ticklish—but it ain't the first ticklish job Casey Ryan ever tackled."

"It can't be did," Barney stated flatly. "An' if it could be did, I wouldn't do it. I ain't as easy t' miss as what you be. I got bulk."

"A hole bored through your tallow might mebbe do you good," Casey suggested harshly. "Might let in a little sand. You can't never tell—"

"My vitals," said Barney with dignity, "is just as close to the surface as what your vitals be. I ain't so fat—I'm big. An' I got all the sand I need. I also have got sense, which some men lacks."

"What yuh figurin' on doin'?" Casey wanted to know. "Set here under a bush an' let 'em pick yuh up same as they would a cottontail, mebbe? We got a hull night to work in, an' Casey's eyes is as good as anybody's in the dark. More'n that, Casey's six-gun kin shoot just as hard an' fast as a rifle—let 'im git close enough."

Barney did not want to be left alone and said so frankly. Neither did he want to climb the butte. He could see no possible gain in climbing to meet an enemy or enemies who could hear the noise of approach. It was plain suicide, he declared, and Barney Oakes was not ready to die.

But Casey could never listen to argument when a fight was in prospect. He filled a canteen, emptied a box of cartridges into his pocket, stuck his old, Colt six-shooter inside his trousers belt, and gave Barney some parting instruction under his breath.

Barney was to move camp down under the bank by the spring, and dig himself in there, so that the only approach would be up the narrow gulch. He would then wait until Casey returned.

"Somebody's after our outfit, most likely," Casey reasoned. "It ain't the first time I've knowed it to happen. So you put the hull outfit outa sight down there an' stand guard over it. If we'd 'a' run when they opened up, they'd uh cleaned us out and left us flat. They's two of us, an' we'll git 'em from two sides."

He stuffed cold bannock into the pocket that did not hold the cartridges and disappeared, climbing the side of the gulch opposite the point which held their ambitious marksman.

To Barney's panicky expostulations he had given little heed. "If yore vitals is as close to your hide as what you claim," Casey had said impatiently, "an' you don't want any punctures in 'em, git to work an' git that hide of yourn outa sight. It'll take some diggin'; they's a lot of yuh to cover."

Barney, therefore, dug like a badger with a dog snuffing at its tail. Casey, on the other hand, climbed laboriously in the darkness a bluff he had not attempted to climb by daylight. It was hard work and slow, for he felt the need of going quietly. What lay over the rim-rock he did not know, though he meant to find out.

Daylight found him leaning against a smooth ledge which formed a part of the black capping he had seen from the road. He had spent the night toiling over boulders and into small gulches and out again, trying to find some crevice through which he might climb to the top. Now he was just about where he had been several hours before, and even Casey Ryan could not help realizing what a fine target he would make if he attempted to climb back down the bluff to camp before darkness again hid his movements.

Standing there puffing and wondering what to do next, he saw the two burros come picking their way toward the spring for their morning drink and a handful apiece of rolled oats which Barney kept to bait them into camp. The lead burro was within easy flinging distance of a rock, from camp, when the thin, unmistakable crack of a rifle-shot came from the right, high up on the rim somewhere beyond Casey. The lead burro pitched forward, struggled to get up, fell again and rolled over, lodging against a rock with its four feet sticking up at awkward angles in the air.

The second burro, always quick to take alarm, wheeled and went galloping away down the draw. But he couldn't outgallop the bullet that sent him in a complete somersault down the slope. Barney might keep the rest of his rolled oats, for the burros were through wanting them.

Casey squinted along the rim of black rock that crested the peak irregularly like a stiff, ragged frill of mourning stuff the gods had thrown away. He could not see the man who had shot the burros. By the intervals between shots, Casey guessed that one man was doing the shooting, though it was probable there were others in the gang. And now that the burros were dead, it became more than ever necessary to locate the gang and have it out with them. That necessity did not worry Casey in the least. The only thing that troubled him now was getting up on the rim without being seen.

It was characteristic of Casey Ryan that, though he moved with caution, he nevertheless moved toward their unseen enemy. Not for a long, long while had Casey been cautious in his behavior, and the necessity galled him. If the hidden marksman had missed that last burro, Casey would probably have taken a longer chance. But to date, every bullet had gone straight to its destination; which was enough to make any man think twice.

Once during the forenoon, while Casey was standing against the rim-rock staring glumly down upon the camp, Barney's hat, perched on a pick handle, lifted its crown above the edge of his hiding place; an old, old trick Barney was playing to see if the rifle were still there and working. The rifle worked very well indeed, for Barney was presently flattened into his retreat, swearing and poking his finger through a round hole in his hat.

Casey seized the opportunity created by the diversion and scurried like a lizard across a bare, gravelly slide that had been bothering him for half an hour. By mid-afternoon he reached a crevice that looked promising enough when he craned up it, but which nearly broke his neck when he had climbed halfway up. Never before had he been compelled to measure so exactly his breadth and thickness. It was drawing matters down rather fine when he was compelled to back down to where he had elbow room, and remove his coat before he could squeeze his body through that crack. But he did it, with his six-shooter inside his shirt and the extra ammunition weighting his trousers pockets.

In spite of his long experience with desert scenery, Casey was somewhat astonished to find himself in a new land, fairly level and with thick groves of pinon cedar and juniper trees scattered here and there. Far away stood other barren hills with deep canyons between. He knew now that the black-capped butte was less a butte than the uptilted nose of a high plateau not half so barren as the lower country. From the pointing Joshua tree it had seemed a peak, but contours are never so deceptive as in the high, broken barrens of Nevada.

He looked down into the gulch where Barney was holed up with their outfit. He could scarcely distinguish the place, it had dwindled so with the distance. He had small hope of seeing Barney. After that last leaden bee had buzzed through his hat crown, you would have to dig faster than Barney if you wanted a look at him. Casey grinned when he thought of it.

When he had gotten his breath and had scraped some loose dirt out of his shirt collar, Casey crouched down behind a juniper and examined his surroundings carefully, his pale, straight-lidded eyes moving slowly as the white, pointing finger of a searchlight while he took in every small detail within view. Midway in the arc of his vision was a ledge, ending in a flat-topped boulder.

The ledge blocked his view, except that he could see trees and a higher peak of rocks beyond it. He made his way cautiously toward the ledge, his eyes fixed upon the boulder. A huge, sloping slab of the granite outcropping it seemed, scaly with gray-green fungus in the cracks where moisture longest remained; granite ledge banked with low junipers warped and stunted and tangled with sage. The longer Casey looked at the boulder, the less he saw that seemed unnatural in a country filled with boulders and outcroppings and stunted vegetation.

But the longer he looked at it, the stronger grew his animal instinct that something was wrong. He waited for a time—a long time indeed for Casey Ryan to wait. There was no stir anywhere save the sweep of the wind blowing steadily from the west.

He crept forward, halting often, eyeing the boulder and its neighboring ledge, distrust growing within him, though he saw nothing, heard nothing but the wind sweeping through branches and bush. Casey Ryan was never frightened in his life. But he was Irish born—and there's something in Irish blood that will not out; something that goes beyond reason into the world of unknown wisdom.

It's a tricksy world, that realm of intuitions. For this is what befell Casey Ryan, and you may account for it as best pleases you.

He circled the rock as a wolf will circle a coiled rattler which it does not see. Beyond the rock, built close against it so that the rear wall must have been the face of the ledge, a little rock cabin squatted secretively. One small window, with two panes of glass was set high under the eaves on the side toward Casey. Cleverly concealed it was, built to resemble the ledge. Visible from one side only, and that was the side where Casey stood. At the back the sloping boulder, untouched, impregnable; at the north and west, a twist of the ledge that hid the cabin completely in a niche. It was the window on the south side that betrayed it.

So here was what the boulder concealed,—and yet, Casey was not satisfied with the discovery. Unconsciously he reached for his gun. This, he told himself, must be the secret habitation of the fiend who shot from rim-rocks with terrible precision at harmless prospectors and their burros.

Casey squinted up at the sun and turned his level gaze again upon the cabin. Reason told him that the man with the rifle was still watching for a pot shot at him and Barney, and that there was nothing whatever to indicate the presence of only one man in the camp below. Had he been glimpsed once during the climb, he would have been fired upon; he would never have been given the chance to gain the top and find this cabin.

The place looked deserted. His practical, everyday mind told him it was empty for the time being. But he felt queer and uncomfortable, nevertheless. He sneaked along the ledge to the cabin, flattened himself against the corner next the gray boulder and waited there for a minute. He felt the flesh stiffening on his jaws as he crept up to the window to look in. By standing on his toes, Casey's eyes came on a level with the lowest inch of glass,—the window was so high.

Just at first Casey could not see much. Then, when his eyes had adjusted themselves to the half twilight within, his mind at first failed to grasp what he saw. Gradually a dimly sensed dread took hold of him, and grew while he stood there peering in at commonplace things which should have given him no feeling save perhaps a faint surprise.

A fairly clean, tiny room he saw, with a rough, narrow bed in one corner and a box table at its head. From the ceiling hung a lantern with the chimney smoked on one side and the warped, pole rafter above it slightly blackened to show how long the lantern had hung there lighted. A door opposite the tiny window was closed, and there was no latch or fastening on the inner side. An Indian blanket covered half the floor space, and in the corner opposite the bed was a queer, drumlike thing of sheet iron with a pipe running through the wall; some heating arrangement, Casey guessed.

In the center of the room, facing the window, a woman sat in a wooden rocking chair and rocked. A pale old woman with dark hollows under her eyes that were fixed upon the pattern of the Indian rug. Her hair was white. Her thin, white hands rested limply on the arms of the chair, and she was rocking back and forth, back and forth, steadily, quietly,—just rocking and staring at the Indian rug.

Casey has since told me that she was the creepiest thing he ever saw in his life. Yet he could not explain why it was so. The woman's face was not so old, though it was lined and without color. There was a terrible quiet in her features, but he felt, somehow, that her thoughts were not quiet. It was as if her thoughts were reaching out to him, telling him things too awful for her thin, hushed lips to let pass.

But after all, Casey's main object was to locate the man with the rifle, and to do it before he himself was seen on the butte. He watched a little longer the woman who rocked and rocked. Never once did her eyes move from that fixed point on the rug. Never once did her fingers move on the arm of the chair. Her mouth remained immobile as the lips of a dead woman. He had to force himself to leave the window; and when he did, he felt guilty, as if he had somehow deserted some one helpless and needing him. He sneaked back, lifted himself and took another long look. The old woman was rocking back and forth, her face quiet with that terrible, pent placidity which Casey could not understand.

Away from the cabin a pebble's throw, he shook his shoulders and pulled his mind away from her, back to the man with the rifle—and to Barney. Rocking in a chair never hurt anybody that he ever heard of. And shooting from rim-rocks did. And Barney was down there, holed up and helpless, though he had grub and water. Casey was up here in a mighty dangerous place without much grub or water but—he hoped—not quite helpless. His immediate, pressing job was not to peek through a high-up window at an old woman rocking back and forth in a chair, but to round up the man who was interfering with Casey's peaceful quest for—well, he called it wealth; but I think that adventure meant more to him.

He picked his way carefully along the edge of the rim-rock, keeping under cover when he could and watching always the country ahead. And without any artful description of his progress, I will simply say that Casey Ryan combed the edge of that rampart for two miles before dark, and found himself at last on the side farthest from Barney without having discovered the faintest trace of any living soul save the woman who rocked back and forth in the little, secret cabin.

Casey sat down on a rock, took a restrained drink from his canteen, and said everything he knew or could invent that was profane and condemnatory of his luck, of the unseen assassin, of the country and his present predicament. He got up, looked all around him, sniffed unavailingly for some tang of smoke in the thin, crisp air, reseated himself and said everything all over again.

Presently he rose and made his way straight across the butte, going slowly to lessen his chance of making a noise for unfriendly ears to hear, and with the stars for guidance.

CHAPTER FOUR

The night was growing cold, and Casey had no coat. At least he could go down and tell Barney what he had discovered and had failed to discover, and get something to eat. Barney would probably be worrying about him, though there was a chance that a bullet had found Barney before dark. Casey was uneasy, and once he was down the fissure again, he hurried as much as possible.

He managed to reach the camp by the little spring without being shot at and without breaking a leg. But Barney was not there. Just at first Casey believed he was dead; but a brief search told Casey that two of the largest canteens were gone, together with a side of bacon, some flour and all of the tobacco. White assassins would have made a more thorough job of robbing the camp. Barney, it was evident, had fled the fate of the burros.

Casey told the stars what he thought of a partner like Barney. Afterward he ate what was easiest to swallow without cooking, overhauled what was left of their outfit, cached the remainder in a clump of bushes, and wearily climbed the bluff again under a capacity load. He concealed himself in the bottom of the fissure to sleep, since he could search no farther.

If he thought wistfully of the palled comfort of his apartment in Los Angeles, and of the Little Woman there, he still did not think strongly enough to send him back to them. For with a canteen or two of water, some food and his two capable legs to carry him, Casey Ryan could have made it to Barstow easily enough. But because he was Casey Ryan, and Irish, and because he was always on the hunt for trouble without recognizing it when he met it in the trail, it never occurred to him to follow Barney down to safer country.

"That there Joshuay tree meant a lot more'n what it let on, pointin' up this way!" Casey muttered, staring down upon a somnolent wilderness blanketed with hushed midnight. "If it thinks it's got Casey whipped, it better think agin and think quick. I'll give it somethin' to point at, 'fore I leave this here butte.

"Funny, the way it kept pointin' up this way. I've saw Joshuays before—miles of 'em. But I never seen one that looked so kinda human and so kinda like it was tryin' to talk. Seems kinda funny; an' that old lady rockin' an' lookin'— seems like her an' the Joshuay has kinda throwed in together, hopin' somebody might come along with savvy enough to kinda—aw, hell!" So did Casey and his Irish belief in the supernatural fall plump against the limitations of his vocabulary.

Against the limitations proscribed by his material predicament, however, Casey Ryan set his face with a grin. Somebody was going to get the big jolt of his life before long, he told himself over a careful breakfast fire built cunningly far back in the crevice where a current of air sucked into the rock capping of the butte. Something was going on up here that shouldn't go on. He did not know what it was, but he meant to stop it. He did not know who was making Indian war on peaceful prospectors, but Casey felt that they were already as good as licked, since he was here with breakfast under his belt and his six-shooter tucked handily inside his waistband.

He squinted up the crack in the ledge, made certain mental alterations in its narrow, jagged walls, and reached for the tough-handled, efficient prospector's pick he had thoughtfully included in his meagre equipment. Slowly and methodically he worked up the crevice, knocking off certain sharp points of rock, and knowing all the while what would probably happen to him if he were overheard.

He was not discovered, however. When he laid elbows on the upper level of the rim and pulled himself up, his coat was on his back where it belonged, and even Barney could have followed him. Yet the top showed no evidence of a widening of the fissure. The bushy junipers hid him completely while he reconnoitred and considered what he should do.

Because the place was close and the invisible call was strong, Casey went first to the rock hut, circled it carefully and found that it was exactly what it had seemed at first sight; a hidden place with no evident opening save that high, small window under the eaves. There was no sign of pathway leading to it, no trace of life outside its wall. But when he crept close and peeked in again, there sat the old woman rocking back and forth. But to-day she stared at the wall before her.

Casey felt a distinct sensation of relief just in knowing that she was, after all, capable of moving. Now her head was not bent, but rested against the back of her chair. She was rocking steadily, quietly, with never a halt.

Casey rapped on the window and waited, fighting a nameless dread of the mystery of her. But she continued to rock and to stare at the wall; if she heard the tapping she gave no sign whatever. So presently he turned away and set himself to the work of finding the man with the rifle.

To that end he first of all climbed the tallest pinon tree in sight; a tree that stood on a rise of ground apart from its brothers. From the concealment of its branches, he surveyed his surroundings carefully, noting especially the notched unevenness of the butte's rim and how just behind him it narrowed unexpectedly to a thin ridge not more than a couple of hundred yards in breadth. A jagged outcropping cut straight across and Casey saw how yesterday he had mistaken that ledge for the rim of the butte. His man must have been out on the point beyond him all the while. He was out there now, very likely; there, or down in the camp he had watched yesterday like a vulture.

His search having narrowed to an area easily covered in an hour or two, Casey turned his head and examined as well as he could the deep canyon that had bitten into the butte and caused that narrow peak. Trees blocked his view there, and he was feeling about for a lower foothold so that he could make the descent when a voice from the ground startled him considerably.

"Come down outa there, before I shoot yuh down!"

Casey looked down and saw what he afterwards declared was the meanest looking man on earth, pointing straight at him the widest muzzled shotgun he had ever seen in his life.

Casey came down. The last ten feet of the distance he made in a clean jump, planting his feet full in the old man's stomach. The meanest looking man on earth gave a grunt and crumpled, with Casey's fingers digging into his throat.

Whether Casey would have killed him or not will never be known. For just as the man was falling limp in his hands, another heavy body landed upon Casey's back. Casey felt a hard, chill circle pressed against his perspiring temple. His hands relaxed and fall away from the throat, leaving finger marks there in the flesh.

"Git up off'n him!" a new voice commanded harshly, and Casey obeyed. His captor shifted the gun muzzle to the back of Casey's neck and poked the gasping, bearded old man with his toe.

"Git up, Paw, you old fool, you! What'd you let 'im light on yuh fer? Why couldn't you a stood back a piece, outa reach? You like to got croaked."

Casey found it prudent to hold his head rather still, as a man does when he carries a boil on his neck. The muzzle of a six-shooter has a quieting effect, when applied to the person by an unfriendly hand. Casey did not at once see the intruder. But presently "Paw" recovered himself and his shotgun, and swung it menacingly toward Casey. Whereupon the cold circle left Casey's medulla oblongata and a long-faced, long-legged youth stepped somewhat hastily to one side.

"Paw, you ol' fool, you, get your finger off'n that trigger whilst you're aimin' at me!" he exclaimed pettishly.

"I wa'n't aimin' at you. I was aimin' at this 'ere—" Casey heard himself called many names, any one of which was good for a fight when Casey was free.

"Aw, you shut up, Paw. You ain't gittin' nobody nowhere," the son interrupted. "You can't cuss 'im t' death—he looks like he could cut loose a few of them pet names hisself if he got a chancet. Yuh might tell us what you was doin' up that there tree, mister. An' what you're doin' on this here butte, anyhow."

Casey looked at him. Knowing Casey, I should say that his eyes were not pleasant. "Talk to Paw," he advised contemptuously. "The two of yuh may possibly be able to stand each other without gittin' sick; but me, I never did git used to skunks!"

That remark very nearly got him a through ticket to Land Beyond. But, being very nearly what Casey had called them, they contented themselves with mouthing vile epithets.

"Better take 'im down to the mine an' keep 'im till Mart gets back, Paw," the long-jawed youth suggested, when he ran short of objurgations. "Mart'll fix 'im when he comes."

"I'd fix 'im, here an', now," threatened Paw, "but Mart, he's so damned techy lately—what we oughta do is bust 'is head with a rock an' pitch 'im over the rim. That'd fix 'im."

They wrangled over the suggestion, and finally decided to take him down and turn him over to one whom they called Joe. Casey went along peaceably, hopeful that he would later have a chance to fight back. He told himself that they both had heads like peanuts, and whenever they moved, he swore, he could hear their brains rattle in their skulls. It doesn't take brains to shoot straight, and he decided that the lanky young man was the one who had shot from the rim-rock. They drove him down into the narrow, deep gulch, following a steep trail that Casey had not seen the day before. The trail led them to the mouth of a tunnel; and by the size of the dump Casey judged that the workings were of a considerable extent. They were getting out silver ore, he guessed, after a glance or two at stray pieces of rock.

Joe was a big, glum-looking individual with his left hand bandaged. He chewed tobacco industriously and maintained a complete silence while Hank, frequently telling Paw to shut up, told how and where they had found Casey spying up on the butte.

"We don't fancy stray desert rats prowlin' around without no reason," said Joe. "Our boss that we're workin' for ain't at home. We're lookin' for 'im back any day now, an' we'll just hold yuh till he comes. He can do as he likes about yuh. You'll have to work fer your board—c'm on an' I'll show yuh how."

Hank followed Casey and Joe into the tunnel. Casey made no objections whatever to going. The tunnel was a fairly long one, he noticed, with drifts opening out of it to left and right. At the end of the main tunnel, Joe turned, took Casey's candle from him and stuck it into a seam in the wall, as he had done with his own.

"Ever drill in rock?" he asked shortly.

"Mebbe I have an' mebbe I ain't," Casey returned defiantly.

"Here's a drill, an' here's your single-jack. Now git t' work. There ain't any loafin' around this camp, and spies never meant good to nobody. Yuh needn't expect to be popular with us—but you'll git your grub if yuh earn it."

Casey looked at the drill, took the double-headed, four-pound hammer and hesitated. He has said that it was pretty hard to resist braining the two of them at once. But there would still be the old man with the shotgun, and he admitted that he was curious about the old woman who rocked and rocked. He decided to wait awhile and see, why these miners found it necessary to shoot harmless prospectors who came near the butte. So he spat into the dust of the tunnel floor, squinted at Joe for a minute and went to work.

That day Casey was kept underground except during the short interval of "shooting" and waiting for the dynamite smoke to clear out of the tunnel; which process Casey assisted by operating a hand blower much against his will. Joe remained always on guard, eyeing Casey suspiciously. When at last he was permitted to pick up his coat and leave the tunnel, night had fallen so that the gulch was dim and shadowy. Casey was conducted to a dugout cabin where bacon was frying too fast and smoking suffocatingly. Paw was there, in a vile temper which seemed to be directed toward the three impartially and to have been caused chiefly by his temporary occupation as camp cook.

Casey watched the old man place food for one person in little dishes which he set in a bake pan for want of a tray. He added a small tin teapot of tea and disappeared from the dugout.

"Two of us waitin' to see your boss, huh?" Casey inquired boldly of Joe. "Can't we eat together?"

"You can call yourself lucky if you eat at all," Joe retorted glumly. "The old man's pretty sore at the way you handled him. He's runnin' this camp; I ain't."

Casey let it go at that, chiefly because he was hungry and tired and did not want to risk losing his supper altogether. Hounds like these, he told himself bitterly, were capable of any crime—from smashing a man's skull and throwing him off the rim-rock to starving him to death. He was Casey Ryan, ready always to fight whether his chance of winning was even or merely microscopical; but even so, Casey was not inclined toward suicide.

When the old man presently returned and the three sat down to the table, Casey obeyed a gesture and sat down with them. In spite of Joe's six-shooter laid handily upon the table beside his plate, Casey ate heartily, though the food was neither well cooked nor over plentiful.

After supper he rose and filled his pipe which they had permitted him to keep. A stranger coming into the cabin might not have guessed that Casey was a prisoner. When the table was cleared and Hank set about washing the dishes, Casey picked up a grimy dish towel branded black in places where it had rubbed sooty kettles, and grinned cheerfully at Paw while he dried a tin plate. Paw eyed him dubiously over a stinking pipe, spat reflectively into the woodbox and crossed his legs the other way, loosely swinging an ill-shod foot.

"Y'ain't told us yet what brung yuh up on the butte," Paw observed suddenly. "Yuh wa'n't lost—yuh ain't got the mark uh no tenderfoot. What was yuh doin' up in that tree?"

"Mebbe I mighta been huntin' mountain sheep," Casey retorted calmly.

"Huntin' mountain sheep up a tree is a new one," tittered Hank. "Wish you'd give me a swaller uh that brand. Must have a kick like a brindle mule."

"More likely 'White Mule.'" Casey cocked a knowing eye at Hank. "You're too late, young feller. I chewed the cork day before yesterday," he declared.

While he fished another plate out of the pan, Casey observed that Paw looked at Joe inquiringly, and that Joe moved his head sidewise a careful inch, and back again.

"Moonshine, huh?" Paw hazarded hopefully. "Yuh peddlin' it, er makin' it?"

Casey grinned secretively. "A man can't be pinched without the goods," he observed shrewdly. "I was raised in a country where they took fools out an' brained 'em with an axe. You fellers ain't been none too friendly, recollect. When's your boss expected home, did yuh say? I'd kinda like to meet 'im."

"He'll kinda like to meet you," Joe returned darkly. "Your actions has been plumb suspicious.

"Nothin' suspicious about MY actions," Casey stated truculently, throwing discretion behind him. "The suspiciousness lays up here somewheres on this butte. If yuh want to know what brung me up here, Casey Ryan's the man that can tell yuh to your faces. I come up here to find out who's been gittin' busy with a high-power on my camp down below. Ain't it natural a man'd want to know who'd shot his two burros—an' 'is pardner?" Casey had impulsively decided to throw in Barney for good measure. "Casey Ryan ain't the man to set under a bush an' be shot at like a rabbit. You can ask anybody if Casey ever backed up fer man er beast. I come up here huntin'. Shore I did. It wasn't sheep I was after—that there's my mistake. It was goats."

"Guess I got yourn," Hank leered "when stuck my gun in your back hair."

"If any one's 'been usin' a high-power it wasn't on this butte," Joe growled. "None uh this bunch done any shootin'. Pap an' Hank, they was up here huntin' burros an I caught yuh up a tree spyin'. We got a little band uh antelope up here we're pertectin'. Our boss got himself made a deppity fer just such cases as yourn appears t' be—pervidin' your case ain't worse.

"Now you say your pardner was shot down below in your camp. That shore looks bad fer you, old-timer. The boss'll shore have t' look into it when he gits here. Lucky we made up our minds t' hold yuh—a murderer, like as not." He filled his pipe with deliberation, while Casey, his jaw sagging, stared from one to the other.

Casey had meant to accuse them to their faces of shooting Barney and the burros from the rim-rock. It had occurred to him that if they believed Barney dead, they might reveal something of their purpose in the attack. Concealment, he felt vaguely, would serve merely to sharpen their suspicion of him. It had seemed very important to Casey that these three should not know that Barney was probably well on his way to Barstow by now.

Barney in Barstow would mean Barney bearing news that Casey Ryan was undoubtedly murdered by outlaws in the Panamints; which would mean a few officers on the trail, with Barney to guide them to the spot. Paw and Hank and Joe—outlaws all, he would have sworn would get what Casey called their needin's. His jaw muscles tightened when he thought of that, and the prospect held him quiet under Joe's injustice.

"I can prove anything I'm asked to prove when the time comes," he said sourly, and began to roll himself a cigarette, since his pipe had gone out. "But I ain't in any courtroom yet, an' you fellers ain't any judge an' jury."

"We got to hold ye," Paw spoke up unctiously, as if the decision had been his. "Ef a crime's been committed, like you say it has, we got to do our duty an' hold ye. The boss'll know what to do with ye—like I said all along; when I hauled ye down outa that tree, for instance."

"Aw, shut up, Paw, you ol' fool, you," Hank commanded again with filial gentleness. "He had yore tongue hangin' out a foot when I come along an' captured 'im. Don't go takin' no credit to yourself—you ain't got none comin'. Mart'll know what to do with 'im, all right. But yuh needn't go an' try to let on to Mart that you was the one that caught 'im. He had you caught. An' he'd a killed yuh if I hadn't showed up an' pulled 'im off'n yuh."

"Well now, when it comes to KILLIN'," Casey interjected spitefully, "I guess I coulda put the two of yuh away if I'd a wanted to right bad. Casey Ryan ain't no killer, because he don't have to be. G'wan an' hold me if yuh feel that way. Grub ain't none too good, but I can stand it till your boss comes. I want a man-to-man talk with him, anyway."

CHAPTER FIVE

That night Casey slept soundly in a bunk built above Joe's bed in the dugout, with Hank and Paw on the opposite side of the room with their guns handy. In the morning he thought well enough of his stomach to get up and start breakfast when Hank had built the fire. He was aware of Joe's suspicious gaze from the lower bunk, and of the close presence of Joe's six-shooter eyeing him balefully from underneath the top blanket. Hank, too, was watchful as a coyote, which he much resembled, in Casey's opinion. But Casey did not mind trifles of that kind, once his mind was at ease about the breakfast and he was free to slice bacon the right thickness, and mix the hot-cake batter himself. For the first time in many weeks he sang—if you could call it singing—over his work.

When Casey Ryan sings over a breakfast fire, you may expect the bacon fried exactly right. You may be sure the hot-cakes will be browned correctly with no uncooked dough inside, and that the coffee will give you heart for whatever hardship the day may hold.

Even Paw's surliness lightened a bit by the time he had speared his tenth cake and walloped it in the bacon grease before sprinkling it thick with sugar and settling the eleventh cake on top. Casey was eyeing the fourteenth cake on Hank's plate when Joe looked up at him over a loaded fork.

"Save out enough dough for three good uns," Joe ordered, "an' fill that little coffee pot an' set it to keep hot, before Hank hogs the hull thing. Dad, seems like you're, too busy t' think uh some things Mart wouldn't want forgot." Paw looked quickly at Casey; but Casey Ryan had played poker all his life, and his weathered face showed no expression beyond a momentary interest, which was natural.

"Other feller hurt bad?" he inquired carelessly, looking at Joe's bandaged hand. He almost grinned when he saw the relieved glances exchanged between Joe and Paw.

"Leg broke," Joe mumbled over a mouthful. "Dad, he set it an' it's doin' all right. He's up in another cabin." Through Hank's brainless titter, Joe added carefully, "Bad ground in the first right-hand drift. We had to abandon it. Rocks big as your head comin' in on yuh onexpected. None uh them right-hand drifts is safe fer a man t' walk in, much less work."

Thereupon Casey related a thrilling story of a cave-in, and assured Joe that he and his partner were lucky to get off with mere broken bones. Casey, you will observe, was running contrary to his nature and leaning to diplomacy.

For himself, I am sure he would never have troubled to placate them. He would have taken the first slim chance that offered—or made one—and fought the three to a finish.

But there was the old woman in the rock hut above them, rocking back and forth and staring at a wall that had no visible opening save one small window to let in the light of outdoors. Prisoner she must be—though why, Casey could only guess.

Perhaps she was some desert woman, the widow of some miner who had been shot as these three had tried to shoot him and Barney Oakes. Mean, malevolent as they were, they would still lack the brutishness necessary to shoot an old woman. So they had shut her up there in the rock hut, not daring to take her back to civilization where she would tell of the crime. It was all plain enough to Casey. The story of the crippled miner made him curl his lip contemptuously when his back was safely turned from Joe.

That day Casey thought much of the old woman in the hut, and of Paw's worse than inferior cooking. Though he did not realize the change in himself, six months of close companionship with the Little Woman had changed Casey Ryan considerably. Time was when even his soft-heartedness would not have impelled him to patient scheming that he might help an old woman whose sole claim upon his sympathy consisted of four rock walls and a look of calm despair in her eyes. Now, Casey was thinking and planning for the old woman more than for himself.

Wherefore, Casey chose the time when he was "putting in an upper" (which is miner's parlance for drilling a hole in the upper face of the tunnel). He gritted his teeth when he swung back the single-jack and landed a glancing blow on the knuckles of his left hand instead of the drill end. No man save Casey Ryan or a surgeon could have told positively whether the metacarpal bones were broken or whether the hand was merely skinned and bruised.

Joe came up, regarded the bleeding hand sourly, led Casey out to the dugout and bandaged the hand for him. There would be no more tunnel work for Casey until the hand had healed; that was accepted without comment.

That night Casey proved to Paw that, with one hand in a sling much resembling Joe's, he could nevertheless cook a meal that made eating a pleasure to look forward to. After that the old woman in the little stone hut had pudding, sometimes, and cake made without eggs, and pie; and the potatoes were mashed or baked instead of plain boiled. Casey had the satisfaction of seeing the dishes return empty to the dugout, and know that he was permitted to add something to her comfort and well-being. The Little Woman would be glad of that, Casey thought with a glow. She might never hear of it, but Casey liked to feel that he was doing something that would please the Little Woman.

For the first few days after Casey was installed as cook, one of the three remained always with him, making it plain that he was under guard. Two were always busy elsewhere. Casey saw that he was expected to believe that they were at work in the tunnel, driving it in to a certain contact of which they spoke frequently and at length.

At supper they would mention their footage for that day's work, and Casey would hide a grin of derision. Casey knew rock as he knew bacon and beans and his sour-dough can. To make the footage they claimed to be making in that tunnel, they would need to shoot twice a day, with a round of, say, five holes to a shot.

As a matter of fact, two holes a day, one shot at noon and one at night, were the most Casey ever heard fired in the tunnel or elsewhere about the mine. But he did not tell them any of the things he thought; not even Joe, who had intelligence far above Paw and Hank, ever guessed that Casey listened every day for their shots and could tell, almost to an inch what progress they were actually making in the tunnel. Nor did he guess that Casey Ryan with his mouth shut was more unsafe than "giant powder" laid out in the sun until it sweated destruction.

Persistent effort, directed by an idea based solely upon an abstract theory, must be driven by a trained intelligence. In this case the abstract theory that every prisoner must be watched must support itself unaided by Casey's behavior. Not even Joe's intelligence was trained to a degree where the theory in itself was sufficient to hold him to the continuous effort of watching Casey.

Wherefore Paw, Hank and Joe presently slipped into the habit of leaving Casey alone for an hour or so; being careful to keep the guns out of his reach, and returning to the dugout at unexpected intervals to make sure that all was well.

Casey Ryan knew his pots and pans, and how to make them fill his days if need be. With savory suppers and his care-free, Casey Ryan grin, he presently lulled them into accepting him as a handy man around camp, and into forgetting that he was at least a potential enemy. Afoot and alone in that unfriendly land, with his left hand smashed and carried in a sling, and on his tongue an Irish joke that implied content with his captivity, Casey Ryan would not have looked dangerous to more intelligent men than these three.

They should have looked one night under the bedding in Casey's bunk. More important still would have been the safeguarding of their "giant powder" and caps and fuse. They should not have left it in a gouged, open hollow under a boulder near the dugout. They were not burdened by the weight of their brains, I imagine.

Just here I should like to say a few words to those who are wholly ignorant of the devastating power contained in "giant powder"—which is dynamite. If you have never had any experience with the stuff, you are likely to go out with a bang and a puff of bluish-brown smoke when you go. On the other hand, you may believe the weird tales one reads now and then, of how whole mountainsides have been thrown down by the discharge of a few sticks of dynamite. Or of one man striking terror to the very souls of a group of mutinous miners by threatening to throw a piece at them. Very well, now this is the truth without any frills of exaggeration or any belittlement:

Dynamite MAY go off by being thrown so that it lands with a jar, but it is not likely to be so hasty as all that. Whole boxes of it have been dropped off wagons traveling over rough trails, with no worse effect than a nervous chill down the spine of the driver of the wagon. It is true that old stuff, after lying around for months and months through varying degrees of temperature, may perform erratically, exploding when it shouldn't and refusing to explode when it should. The average miner refuses to take a chance with stale "giant" if he can get hold of fresh.

One stick the size of an ordinary candle, and from that to a maximum amount of four sticks, may be used to "load" a hole eighteen to twenty-four inches long, drilled into living rock. The amount of dynamite used depends upon the quality of rock to be broken and the skill and good judgment of the miner. In average hard-rock mining, from three to five of these holes are drilled in a space four-by-six feet in area.

A stick of dynamite is exploded by inserting in one end of the stick a high-power detonating cap which will deliver a twenty-pound blow per X—whatever that means. From three- to six-X caps are used in ordinary mining. Three-X caps sometimes fail to explode a stick of dynamite. A six-X cap, delivering a one-hundred-and-twenty-pound blow, may be counted upon to do the work without fail.

The cap itself is exploded by a spark running through a length of fuse, the length depending altogether upon the time required to reach a point of safety after the fuse is lighted. The cap is really more dangerous to handle than is the dynamite itself. The cap is a tricky thing that may go off at any jar or scratch or at a spark from pipe or cigarette. You can, if you are sufficiently careless of possible results, light the twisted paper end of a stick of dynamite and watch the dynamite burn like wax in your fingers; it MAY go off and set your friends to work retrieving portions of your body. More likely, it will do nothing but burn harmlessly.

Well, then, a piece of fuse is inserted in the open end of the cap, and the metal pressed tight against the fuse to hold it in place. Pressed down by the miner's teeth, sometimes, if he has been long in the business and has grown careless about his head; otherwise he crimps the cap on with a small pair of pliers or the back of his knife blade—and feels a bit easier when it is done without losing a hand.

You would think, unless you are accustomed to the stuff, that when five holes are loaded with, probably, ten or twelve sticks of dynamite to the lot, each hole containing a six-X exploding cap as well, that the first shot would likewise be the last shot and that the whole tunnel would cave in and the mountain behind it would shake. Nothing like that occurs. If there are five loaded holes in the tunnel face, and you do not hear, one after the other, five muffled BOOMS, you will know that one hole failed to go off—and that the miner is worried. It happens sometimes that four holes loaded with eight sticks of dynamite explode within a foot or so of the fifth hole and yet the fifth hole remains "dead" and a menace to the miner until it is discharged.

So please don't swallow those wild tales of a stick of dynamite that threw down a mountainside. I once read a story—it was not so long ago—of a Chinaman who wiped out a mine with a little piece of dynamite which he carried in his pocket. I laughed.

Casey Ryan, on the first day when he was left alone with his crippled hand and his pots and pans for company, did nothing whatever that he would not have done had one of the three been present. He was suspicious of their going and thought it was a trap set to catch him in an attempted escape.

On the second day when the three went off together and left him alone, Casey went out gathering wood and discovered just where the "powder," fuse and caps were kept under a huge, black boulder between the tunnel portal and the dugout. On the third day he also gathered wood and helped himself to two sticks of dynamite, three caps and eighteen inches of fuse. Not enough to be missed unless they checked their supply more carefully than Casey believed they did; but enough for Casey's purpose nevertheless.

That night, while the moon shone in through the dingy window at the head of his bunk and gave him a little light to work by, Casey sat up in bed and snored softly and with a soothing rhythm while he cut a stick of dynamite in two, capped five inches of fuse for each piece working awkwardly with his one good hand and pinching the caps tight with his teeth, which might have sent him with a bang into Kingdom Come—and very carefully worked the caps into the powder until no more than three inches of fuse protruded from the end of the half stick. It would have been less dangerous to land with a yell in the middle of the floor and fight the three men with one bare hand, but Casey's courage never turned a hair.

Still snoring mildly, he held up to the moonlight two deadly weapons and surveyed them with much satisfaction. They would not be so quick, as fiction would have them, but if his aim was accurate in throwing, they would be deadly enough. Moreover, he could count with a good deal of certainty upon a certain degree of terror which the sight of them in his hand would produce.

When Casey Ryan cooked breakfast next morning, he carried two half-sticks of loaded dynamite under his hand in the sling. Can you wonder that even he shied at standing over the stove cooking hot cakes and complained that his broken hand pained him a lot and that the heat made it worse? But a shrewd observer would have noticed on his face the expression of a cat that has been shut in the pantry over night.

Joe volunteered to take another look at the hand and see if blood poison was "setting in"; but Casey said it didn't feel like blood poison. He had knocked it against the bunk edge in his sleep, he declared. He'd dose 'er with iodine after a while, and she'd be all right.

Joe let it go at that, being preoccupied with other matters at which Casey could only guess. He conferred with Paw outside the dugout after breakfast, called Hank away from the dish-washing and the three set off toward the tunnel with a brisker air than usually accompanied them to work. Casey watched them go and felt reasonably sure of at least two hours to himself.

The first thing Casey did after he had made sure that he was actually alone was to remove the deadly stuff from the sling and lay it on a shadowed shelf where it would be safe but convenient to his hand. Then, going to his bunk, he reached under the blankets and found the other stick of dynamite which he had not yet loaded. This he laid on the kitchen table and cut it in two as he had done last night with the other stick. With his remaining cap he loaded a half and carried it back to his bunk. He was debating in his mind whether it was worth while purloining another cap from a box under the boulder when another fancy took him and set him grinning.

Four separate charges of dynamite, he reasoned, would not be necessary. It was an even chance that the sight of a piece with the fuse in his hand would be sufficient to tame Paw or Hank or Joe—or the three together, for that matter—without going further than to give them a sight of it.

With that idea uppermost, Casey split the paper carefully down the side of the remaining half-stick, took out the contents in a tin plate and carried it outside where he buried it in the sand beneath a bush. Returning to the dugout he made a thick dough of leftover pancake batter and molded it into the dynamite wrapping with a fragment of harmless fuse protruding from the opened end. When the thing was dry, Casey thought it would look very deadly and might be useful. After several days of helplessness for want of a weapon, Casey was in a mood to supply himself generously.

He finished the dish-washing, working awkwardly with one hand. After that he put a kettle of beans on to boil, filled the stove with pinon sticks and closed the drafts. He armed himself with the two loaded pieces of dynamite from the cupboard, filled his pockets with such other things as he thought he might need, and went prospecting on his own account.

At the portal of the tunnel he stopped and listened for the ping-g, ping-g of a single-jack striking steadily upon steel. But the tunnel was silent, the ore car uptilted at the end of its track on the dump. Yet the three men were supposedly at work in the mine, had talked at breakfast about wanting to show a certain footage when the boss returned, and of needing to hurry.

Casey went into the tunnel, listening and going silently; sounds travel far in underground workings. At the mouth of the first right-hand drift he stopped again and listened. This, if he would believe Joe, was the drift where the bad ground had caused the accident to Joe and his partner whose leg had been broken. Casey found the drift as silent as the main tunnel. He went in ten feet or so and lighted the candle he had pulled from inside his shirt. With the candle held in the swollen fingers of his injured hand, and a prospector's pick taken from the portal in his other, Casey went on cautiously, keeping an eye upon the roof which, to his wise, squinting eyes, looked perfectly solid and safe.

If a track had ever been laid in this drift it had long since been removed. But a well-defined path led along its center with boot tracks going and coming, blurring one another with much passing. Casey grinned and went on, his ears cocked for any sound before or behind, his shoes slung over his arm by their tied laces.

So he came, in the course of a hundred feet or so, to a crude door of split cedar slabs, the fastening padlocked on his side. Casey had vaguely expected some such bar to his path, and he merely gave a grunt of satisfaction that the lock was old and on his side of the door.

With his jackknife Casey speedily took off one side of the lock and opened it. Making the door appear locked behind him when he had passed through was a different matter, and Casey did not attempt it. Instead, he merely closed the door behind him, carrying the padlock in with him.

As Casey reviewed his situation, being on the butte at all was a risk in itself. One detail more or less could not matter so much. Besides, he was a bold Casey Ryan with two loaded half-sticks of dynamite in his sling.

A crude ladder against the wall of a roomy stope beyond the door did not in the least surprise him. He had expected something of this sort. When he had topped the ladder and found himself in a chamber that stretched away into blackness, he grunted again his mental confirmation of a theory working out beautifully in fact. His candle held close to the wall, he moved forward along the well-trodden path, looking for a door. Mechanically he noticed also the formation of the wall and the vein of ore—probably high-grade in pockets, at least—that had caused this chamber to be dug. The ore, he judged, had long since been taken out and down through the stope into the tunnel and so out through the main portal. These workings were old and for mining purposes abandoned. But just now Casey was absorbed in solving the one angle of the mystery which he had stumbled upon at first, and he gave no more than a glance and a thought to the silent testimony of the rock walls.

He found the door, fastened also on the outside just as he had expected it would be. Beside it stood a rather clever heating apparatus which Casey did not examine in detail. His Irish heart was beating rather fast while he unfastened the door. Beyond that door his thoughts went questing eagerly but he hesitated nevertheless before he lifted his knuckles and rapped.

There was no reply. Casey waited a minute, knocked again, then pulled the door open a crack and looked in. The old woman sat there rocking back and forth, steadily, quietly. But her thin fingers were rolling a corner of her apron hem painstakingly, as if she meant to hem it again. Her eyes were fixed absently upon the futile task. Casey watched her as long as he dared and cleared his throat twice in the hope that she would notice him. But the old woman rocked back and forth and rolled her apron hem; unrolled it and carefully rolled it again.

"Good morning, ma'am," said Casey, clearing his throat for the third time and coming a step into the room with his candle dripping wax on the floor.

For just an instant the uneasy fingers paused in their rolling of the apron hem. For just so long the rockers hesitated in their motion. But the old woman did not reply nor turn her face toward him; and Casey pushed the door shut behind him and took two more steps toward her.

"I come to see if yuh needed anything, ma'am; a friend, mebbe." Casey grinned amiably, wanting to reassure her if it were possible to make her aware of his presence. "They had yuh locked in, ma'am. That don't look good to Casey Ryan. If yuh wanta get out—if they got yuh held a prisoner here, or anything like 'that, you can trust Casey Ryan any old time. Is—can I do anything for yuh, ma'am?" The old woman dropped her hands to her lap and held them there, closely clasped. Her head swung slowly round until she was looking at Casey with that awful, fixed stare she had heretofore directed at the wall or the floor.

"Tell those hell-hounds they have a thousand years to burn—every one of them!" she said in a deep, low voice that had in it a singing resonance like a chant. "Every cat, every rat, every mouse, every louse, has a thousand year's to burn. Tell Mart the hounds of hell must burn!" Her voice carried a terrible condemnation far beyond the meaning of the words themselves. It was as if she were pronouncing the doom of the whole world. "Every cat, every rat, every mouse, every louse—"

Casey Ryan's jaw dropped an inch. He backed until he was against the door. He had to swallow twice before he could find his voice, and those of you who know Casey Ryan will appreciate that. He waited until she had finished her declaration.

"No, ma'am, you're wrong. I come up here to see if I could help yuh."

"Hounds of hell—black as the bottomless pit that spewed you forth to prey upon mankind! The world will have to burn. Tell those hounds of hell that bay at the gibbous moon the world will have to burn. Every cat, every rat, every mouse, every louse has a thousand years to burn!"

Casey Ryan, with his mouth half open and his eyes rather wild, furtively opened the door behind him. Still meeting fixedly the dull glare of the old woman's eyes, Casey slid out through the door and fastened it hastily behind him. With an uneasy glance now and then over his shoulder as if he feared the old woman might be in pursuit of him, he hurried back down the ladder to the closed door in the drift, pulled the door shut behind him and put the padlock in place before he breathed naturally.

He stopped then to put on his shoes, made his way to the drift opening and listened again for voices or footsteps. When he found the way clear he hurried out and back to the dugout. The first thing he did was to fill his pipe and light it. Even then the sonorous voice of the old woman intoning her dreadful proclamation against the world rang in his ears and sent occasional ripples of horror down his spine. Seen through the window, she had looked a sad, lonely old lady who needed sympathy and help. At closer range she was terrible. Casey was trying to forget her by busying himself about the stove when Joe walked in unexpectedly.

Joe stood just inside the door, staring at Casey with a glassy look in his eyes. Something in Joe's face warned Casey of impending events; but with that terrible old woman still fresh in his mind, Casey was in the mood to welcome distraction of any sort. He shifted his hand in the sling so that his concealed weapons lay more comfortably therein, secure from detection, and waited.

Joe leaned forward, lifted an arm slowly and aimed a finger at Casey accusingly.

"Pap says that you're a Federal officer!" he began, waggling his finger at Casey. "Pap thinks you come here spyin' around t' see what we're up to on this here butte. Now, you can't pull nothin' like that! You can't get away with it.

"Hank, he wants t' bump yuh off an' say nothin' to anybody. Now, I come t' have it out with yuh. If you're a Federal officer we're goin' t' settle with yuh an' take no chances. Mart, he's more easy-goin' in some ways, on account of havin' his crazy ol' mother on 'is hands t' take care of. Mart don't want no killin'—on account of his mother goin' loony when 'is dad got killed. But Mart ain't here. Pap an' Hank, they been at me all mornin' t' let 'em bump yuh off.

"But Pap an' Hank, they're drunk, see? I'm the only sober man left on the job. So I come up here t' settle with yuh myself. Takes a sober man with a level head t' settle these things. Now, if you come up here spyin' an' snoopin', you git bumped off an' no argument about it. Mart's got his mother t' take care of— an' we aim t' pertect Mart. If you're a Federal officer, I want t' know it here an' now. If yuh ain't, I want yuh t' sample some uh the out-kickin'est 'White Mule' yuh ever swallered. Now which are yuh, and what yuh goin' t' do? I want my answer here an' now, an' no argument an' no foolin'!"

Casey blinked but his mouth widened in a grin. "Me, I never went lookin' fer nothin, I wouldn't put under my vest, Joe," he declared convincingly. So that was it! He was thinking against time. Moonshiners as well as would-be murderers they were—and Joe drunk and giving them away like a fool. Casey wished that he knew where Hank and Paw were at this moment. He hoped, too, that Joe was right—that Hank and Paw were drunk. He'd have the three of them tied in a row before dark, in any case. The thing to do now was to humor Joe along—leave it to Casey Ryan!

Joe was uncorking a small, flat bottle of pale liquor. Now he held it out to Casey. Casey took it, thinking he would pretend to drink, would urge Joe to take a drink; it would be simple, once he got Joe started. But Joe had a few ideas of his own concerning the celebration. He pulled a gun unexpectedly, leaned against the closed door to steady himself and aimed it full at Casey.

"In just two minutes I'm goin' t' shoot if that there bottle ain't empty," he stated gravely, nodding his head with intense pride in his ability to handle the situation. "If you're a Federal officer, yuh won't dast t' drink. If yuh ain't, you'll be almighty glad to. Anyway, it'll be settled one way or t'other. Drink 'er down!"

Casey blinked again, but this time he did not grin. He debated swiftly his chance of scaring Joe with the dynamite before Joe would shoot. But Joe had his finger crooked with drunken solemnity upon the trigger. The time for dynamite was not now.

"Pap an' Hank, they lap up anything an' call it good. I claim that's got a back-action kick to it. Drink 'er down!"

Casey drank 'er down. It was like swallowing flames. It was a half-pint flask, and it was full when Casey, with Joe's eyes fixed upon him, tilted it and began to drink. Under Joe's baleful glare Casey emptied the flask before he stopped.

Joe settled his shoulders comfortably against the doorway and watched Casey make for the water bucket.

"I claim that's the out-kickin'est stuff that ever was made on Black Butte. How'd yuh like it?"

"All right," Casey bore witness, keeping his eyes fixed on Joe and the gun and trying his best to maintain a nonchalant manner. "I'd call it purty fair hootch."

"It's GOOD hootch!" Joe declared impressively, apparently quite convinced that Casey was not a Federal officer. "Can yuh feel the kick'to it?"

Casey backed until he sat on the edge of the table his good right hand supporting his left elbow outside the sling. He grinned at Joe and while he still keenly realized that he was playing a part for the sole purpose of gaining somehow an advantage over Joe, he was conscious of a slight giddiness. An unprejudiced observer would have noticed that his grin was not quite the old, Casey Ryan grin. It was a shade foolish.

"Bet your life I can feel the kick!" he agreed, nodding his head. "You can ask anybody." Then Casey discovered something strange in Joe's appearance. He lifted his head, held it very still and regarded Joe attentively.

"Say, Joe, what yuh tryin' to do with that six-gun? Tryin' to write your name in the air with it?"

Joe looked inquiringly down at the gun, eyeing it as if it were a new and absolutely unknown object. He satisfied himself apparently beyond all doubt that the gun was doing nothing it should not do, and finally turned his attention to Casey sitting on the table and grinning at him meaninglessly.

"Ain't writin' nothin'," Joe stated solemnly. "It's yore eyes. Gun's all right— yo'r seein' crooked. It's the hootch. Back-action kick to it. Ain't that right?"

"That's right," nodded Casey and he added, grinning more foolishly, "Darn right, that's right! Back-action kick—bet your life."

Joe pushed the gun inside his waistband and crooked his finger at Casey, beckoning mysteriously. "C'mon an' I'll show yuh how it's made," he invited with heavy enthusiasm. "Yore a judge uh hootch all right—I can see that. I'll show yuh how we do it. Best White Mule in Nevada. Ain't that right? Ain't that the real hootch?"

"'S right, all right," Casey agreed earnestly. "Puttin' the hoot in hootch—you fellers. You can ask anybody if that ain't right."

Joe laughed hoarsely. "Puttin' the hoot in hootch—that's right. I knowed you was all right. Didn't I say you was? I told Hank an' Pap you wasn't no Federal officer. They know it, too. I was foolin' back there. I knowed you didn't need no gun pulled on yuh t' make yuh put away the hootch. Lapped it up like a thirsty hound. I knowed yuh would—I was kiddin' yuh, runnin' that razoo with the gun. Ain't that right?"

"Darn right, that's right! I knew you was foolin' all along. You knew Casey Ryan's all right—sure, you knowed it!" Casey laid his good hand investigatively against his stomach. "Pretty hot hootch—you can ask anybody if it ain't! Workin' like an air drill a'ready."

He blinked inquisitively at Joe, who stared back inquiringly. "Who's your friend?" Casey demanded pugnaciously. "He sneaked in on yuh. I never seen 'im come in."

Joe turned slowly and looked behind him at the blank boards of the unpainted door. Just as slowly he turned back to Casey. A slow grin split his leathery face.

"Ain't nobody. It's the hootch. Told yuh, didn't I? Gittin' the best of yuh, ain't it? C'mon—I'll show yuh how it's made."

"Take a barr'l t' git the besta—Casey Ry'n," Casey boasted, his words blurring noticeably. "Where's y'r White Mule? Let 'er kick—Casey Ry'n can lead 'er an' tame 'er—an' make'r eat outa 's hand!" Following Joe, Casey stepped high over a rock no bigger than his fist.

With a lurch he straightened and tried to pull his muddled wits out of the fog that was fast enveloping them. Dimly he sensed the importance of this discovery which Joe had forced upon him. In flashes of normalcy he knew that he must see all he could of their moonshine operations. He must let them think he was drunk until he knew all their secrets. He assured himself vaguely that he must, above all things, keep his head.

But it was all pretty hazy and rapidly growing hazier. Casey Ryan, you must know, was not what is informally termed a drinking man. In his youth he might have been able to handle a sudden half-pint of moonshine whisky and keep as level a head as he now strove valiantly to retain. But Casey's later years had been more temperate than most desert men would believe. Unfortunately virtue is not always it own reward; at least Casey now found himself the worse for past abstinences.

Joe led him into the tunnel, laughing sardonically because Casey found it scarcely wide enough for his oscillating progress. They turned into a drift. Casey did not know which drift it was, though he tried foggily to remember. He was still, you must know, trying to keep a level head and gain valuable information for the sheriff who he hoped would return to the butte with Barney.

Paw and Hank were wrangling somewhere ahead. Casey could hear their raised voices mingled in a confused rumbling in the pent walls of the drift. Casey thought they passed through a doorway, and that Joe closed a heavy door behind them, but he was not sure.

Memory of the old woman intoning her horrible anathema surged back upon Casey with the closing of the door. The voices of Hank and Paw he now mistook for the ravings of the woman in the stone hut. Casey balked there, and would not go on. He did not want to face the old woman again, and he said so repeatedly—or believed that he did.

Joe caught him by the arm and pulled him forward by main strength. The voices of Paw and Hank came closer and clarified into words; or did Casey and Joe walk farther and come into their presence?

They were all standing together somewhere, in a large, underground chamber with a hole letting in the sunlight high up on one side. Casey was positive there was a hole up there, because the sun shone in his eyes and to avoid it he moved aside and fell over a bucket or a keg or something. Hank laughed loudly at the spectacle, and Paw swore because the fall startled him; but it was Joe who helped Casey up.

Casey knew that he was sitting on a barrel—or something—and telling a funny story. He thought it must be very funny indeed, because every one was laughing and bending double and slapping legs while he talked. Casey realized that here at last were men who appreciated Casey Ryan as he deserved to be appreciated. Tears ran down his own weathered cheeks—tears of mirth. He had never laughed so much before in all his life, he thought. Every one, even Paw, who was normally a mean, cantankerous old cuss, was having the time of his life.

They attempted to show Casey certain intricacies of their still, which made it better than other stills and put a greater kick in the White Mule it bred. Somewhere back in the dim recesses of Casey's mind, he felt that he ought to listen and remember what they told him. Vaguely he knew that he must not take another drink, no matter how insistent they were. In the brief glow of that resolution Casey protested that he could hoot without any more hootch. But he hated to hurt Paw's feelings, or Hank's or Joe's. They had made the hootch with a new and different twist, and they were honestly anxious for his judgment and approval. He decided that perhaps he really ought to take a little more just to please them; not much—a couple of drinks maybe. Wherefore, he graciously consented to taste the "run" of the day before. Thereafter Casey Ryan hooted to the satisfaction of everybody, himself most of all.

After an indeterminate interval the four left the still, taking a bottle with them so that it might be had without delay, should they meet a snake or a hydrophobia skunk or some other venomous reptile. It was Casey who made the suggestion, and he became involved in difficulties when he attempted the word venomous. Once started Casey was determined to pronounce the word and pronounce it correctly, because Casey Ryan never backed up when he once started. The result was a peculiar humming which accompanied his reeling progress down the drift (now so narrow that Casey scraped both shoulders frequently) to the portal.

They stopped on the flat of the dump and argued over the advisability of taking a drink apiece before going farther, as a sort of preventive. Joe told them solemnly that they couldn't afford to get drunk on the darn' stuff. It had too hard a back-action kick, he explained, and they might forget themselves if they took too much. It was important, Joe explained at great length, that they should not forget themselves. The boss had always impressed upon them the grim necessity of remaining sober whatever happened.

"We never HAVE got drunk," Joe reiterated, "and we can't afford t' git drunk now. We've got t' keep level heads, snakes or no snakes."

Casey Ryan's head was level. He wabbled up to Joe and told him so to his face, repeating the statement many times and in many forms. He declaimed it all the way up the path to the dugout, and when they were standing outside. Beyond all else, Casey was anxious that Joe should feel perfectly certain that he, Casey Ryan, knew what he was doing, knew what he was saying, and that his head was and always had been perr-rf'c'ly level-l-l.

"Jus' t' prove-it—I c'n kill that jack-over-there—without-no-gun!" Casey bragged bubblingly, running his words together as if they were being poured in muddy liquid from his mouth. "B'lieve it? Think-I-can't?"

The three turned circumspectly and stared solemnly at a gray burro with a crippled front leg that had limped to the dump heap within easy throwing distance from the cabin door. Hobbling on three legs it went nosing painfully amongst a litter of tin cans and bent paper cartons, hunting garbage. As if conscious that it was being talked about, the burro lifted its head and eyed the four mournfully, its ears loosely flopping.

"How?" questioned Paw, waggling his beard disparagingly. "Spit 'n 'is eye?"

"Talk 'm t' death," Hank guessed with imbecile shrewdness.

"Think-I-can't? What'll—y'bet?"

They disputed the point with drunken insistence and mild imprecations, Hank and Paw and Joe at various times siding impartially for and against Casey. Casey gathered the impression that none of them believed him. They seemed to think he didn't know what he was talking about. They even questioned the fact that his head was level. He felt that his honor was at stake and that his reputation as a truthful man and a level-headed man was threatened.

While they wrangled, the fingers of Casey's right hand fumbled unobserved in the sling on his left, twisting together the two short lengths of fuse so that he might light both as one piece. Even in his drunkenness Casey knew dynamite and how best to handle it. Judgment might be dethroned, but the mechanical details of his profession were grooved deep into habit and were observed automatically and without the aid of conscious thought.

He braced himself against the dugout wall and raised his hand to the cigarette he had with some trouble rolled and lighted. A spitting splutter arose, that would have claimed the attention of the three, had they not been unanimously engaged in trying to out-talk one another upon the subject of Casey's ability to kill a burro seventy-five feet away without a gun.

Casey glanced at them cunningly, drew back his right hand and pitched something at the burro.

"Y' watch 'im!" he barked, and the three turned around to look, with no clear conception of what it was they were expected to watch.

The burro jerked its head up, then bent to sniff at the thin curl of powder smoke rising from amongst the cans. Paw and Hank and Joe were lifted some inches from the ground with the explosion. They came down in a hail of gravel, tin cans and fragments of burro. Casey, flattened against the wall in preparation for the blast, laughed exultantly.

Paw and Hank and Joe picked themselves up and clung together for mutual support and comfort. They craned necks forward, goggling incredulously at what little was left of the burro and the pile of tin cans.

"'Z that a bumb?" Paw cackled nervously at last, clawing gravel out of his uncombed beard. "'Z got me all shuck up. Whar's that 'r bottle?"

"'Z goin' t' eat a bumb—ol' fool burro!" Hank chortled weakly, feeling tenderly certain nicks on his cheeks where gravel had landed. "Paw, you ol' fool, you, don't hawg the hull thing—gimme a drink!"

"Casey's sure all right," came Joe's official O.K. of the performance. "Casey said 'e c'd do it—'n' Casey done it!" He turned and slapped Casey somewhat uncertainly on the back, which toppled him against the wall again. "Good'n on us, Casey! Darn' good joke on us—'n' on the burro!"

Whereupon they drank to Casey solemnly, and one and all, they proclaimed that it was a VERY good joke on the burro. A merciful joke, certainly; as you would agree had you seen the poor brute hungry and hobbling painfully, hunting scraps of food amongst the litter of tin cans.

After that, Casey wanted to sleep. He forced admissions from the three that he, Casey Ryan, was all right and that he knew exactly what he was doing and kept a level head. He crawled laboriously into his bunk, shoes, hat and all; and, convinced that he had defended his honor and preserved the Casey Ryan reputation untarnished, he blissfully skipped the next eighteen hours.

CHAPTER SIX

Casey awoke under the vivid impression that some one was driving a gadget into his skull with a "double-jack." The smell of bacon scorching filled his very soul with the loathing of food. The sight of Joe calmly filling his pipe roused Casey to the fighting mood—with no power to fight. He was a sick man; and to remain alive was agony.

The squalid disorder and the stale aroma of a drunken orgy still pervaded the dugout and made it a nightmare hole to Casey. Hank came tittering to the bunk and offered him a cup of coffee, muddy from too long boiling, and Joe grinned over his pipe at the colorful language with which Casey refused the offering.

"Better take a brace uh hootch," Joe suggested with no more than his normal ill nature. "I got some over at the still we made awhile back that, ain't quite so kicky. Been agin' it in wood an' charcoal. That tones 'er down. I'll go git yuh some after we eat. Kinda want a brace, myself. That new hootch shore is a kickin' fool."

Paw accepted this remark, as high praise, and let three hot cakes burn until their edges curled while he bragged of his skill as a maker of moonshine. Paw himself was red-eyed and loose-lipped from yesterday's debauch. Hank's whole face, especially in the region of his eyes, was puffed unbecomingly. Casey, squinting an angry eye at Hank and the cup of coffee, spared a thought from his own misery to acknowledge surprise that anything on earth could make Hank more unpleasant to look upon. Joe had a sickly pallor to prove the potency of the brew.

For such is the way of moonshine when fusel oil abounds, as it does invariably in new whisky distilled by furtive amateurs working in secret and with neither the facilities nor the knowledge for its scientific manufacture. There is grim significance in the sardonic humor of the man who first named it White Mule. The kick is certain and terrific; frequently it is fatal as well. The worst of it is, you never know what the effect will be until you have drunk the stuff; and after you have drunk it, you are in no condition to resist the effect or to refrain from courting further disaster.

That is what happened to Casey. The poison in the first half-pint, swallowed under the eye of Joe's six-shooter, upset his judgment. The poison in his further potations made a wholly different man of Casey Ryan; and the after effect was so terrific that he would have swallowed cyanide if it promised relief.

He gritted his teeth and suffered tortures until Joe returned and gave him a drink of whisky in a chipped granite cup. Almost immediately he felt better. The pounding agony in his head eased perceptibly and his nerves ceased to quiver. After a while he sat up, gazed longingly at the water bucket and crawled down from the bunk. He drank largely in great gulps. His bloodshot eyes strayed meditatively to the coffee pot. After an undecided moment he walked uncertainly to the stove and poured himself a cup of coffee.

Casey lifted the cup to drink, but the smell of it under his nose sickened him. He weaved uncertainly to the door, opened it and threw out the coffee—cup and all. Which was nature flying a storm flag, had any one with a clear head been there to observe the action and the look on Casey's face.

"Gimme another shot uh that damn' hootch," he growled. Joe pushed the bottle toward Casey, eyeing him curiously.

"That stuff they run yesterday shore is kicky," Joe ruminated sympathetically. "Pap's proud as pups over it. He thinks it's the real article—but I dunno. Shore laid yuh out, Casey, an' yuh never got much, neither. Not enough t' lay yuh out the way it did. Y' look sick."

"I AM sick!" Casey snarled, and poured himself a drink more generous than was wise. "When Casey Ryan says he's sick, you can put it down he's SICK! He don't want nobody tellin' 'im whether 'e's sick 'r not.—he KNOWS 'e's sick!" He drank, and swore that it was rotten stuff not fit for a hawg (which was absolute truth). Then he staggered to the stove, picked up the coffee pot, carried it to the door and flung it savagely outside because the odor offended him.

"Mart got back last night," Joe announced casually. "You was dead t' the world. But we told 'im you was all right, an' I guess he aims t' give yuh steady work an' a cut-in on the deal. We been cleanin' up purty good money—but Mart says the market ain't what it was; too many gone into the business. You're a good cook an' a good miner an' a purty good feller all around—only the boss says you'll have t' cut out the booze."

"'J you tell 'im you MADE me drink it?" Casey halted in the middle of the floor, facing Joe indignantly.

"I told 'im I put it up t' yuh straight—what your business is, an' all. You got no call t' kick—didn't I go swipe this bottle uh booze for yuh t' sober up on, soon as the boss's back was turned? I knowed yuh needed it; that's why. We all needed it. I'm just tellin' yuh the boss don't approve of no celebrations like we had yest'day. I got up early an' hauled that burro outa sight 'fore he seen it. That's how much a friend I be, an' it wouldn't hurt yuh none to show a little gratitude!"

"Gratitude, hell! A lot I got in life t' be grateful for!" Casey slumped down on the nearest bench, laid his injured hand carefully on the table and leaned his aching head on the other while he discoursed bitterly on the subject of his wrongs.

His muddled memory fumbled back to his grievance against traffic cops, distorting and magnifying the injustice he had received at their hands. He had once had a home, a wife and a fortune, he declared, and what had happened? Laws and cops had driven him out, had robbed him of his home and his family and sent him out in the hills like a damned kiotey, hopin' he'd starve to death. And where, he asked defiantly, was the gratitude in that?

He told Joe ramblingly but more or less truthfully how he had been betrayed and deserted by a man he had befriended; one Barney Oakes, upon whom Casey would like to lay his hands for a minute.

"What I done to the burro ain't nothin' t' what I'd do t' that hound uh hell!" he declared, pounding the table with his good fist.

Homeless, friendless; but Joe was his friend, and Paw and Hank were his friends—and besides them there was in all the world not one friend of Casey Ryan's. They were good friends and good fellows, even if they did put too much hoot in their hootch. Casey Ryan liked his hootch with a hoot in it.

He was still hooting (somewhat incoherently it is true, with recourse now and then to the bottle because he was sick and he didn't give a darn who knew it) when the door opened and he whom they called Mart walked in. Joe introduced him to Casey, who sat still upon the bench and looked him over with drunken disparagement. Casey had a hazy recollection of wanting to see the boss and have it out with him, but he could not recall what it was that he had been so anxious to quarrel about.

Mart was a slender man of middle height, with thin, intelligent face and a look across the eyes like the old woman who rocked in the stone hut. He glanced from the bottle to Casey, eyeing him sharply. Drunk or sober, Casey was not the man to be stared down; nevertheless his fingers strayed involuntarily to his shirt collar and pulled fussily at the wrinkles.

"So you're the man they've been holding here for my inspection," Mart said coolly, with a faint smile at Casey's evident discomfort. "You're still hitting it up, I see. Joe, take that bottle away from him. When he's sober enough to talk straight, I'll give him the third degree and see what he really is, anyway. Guess he's all right—but he sure can lap up the booze. That's a point against him."

Casey's hand went to the bottle, beating Joe's by three inches. He did not particularly want the whisky, but it angered him to hear Mart order it taken from him. Away back in his mind where reason had gone into hiding, Casey knew that some great injustice was being done him; that he, Casey Ryan, was not the man they were calmly taking it for granted that he was.

With the bottle in his hand he rose and walked unsteadily to his bunk. He did not like this man they called the boss. He remembered that in his bunk, under the bedding, he had concealed something that would make him the equal of them all. He fumbled under the blankets, found what he sought and with his back turned to the others he slipped the thing into his sling out of sight.

Mart and Joe were talking together by the table, paying no attention to Casey, who was groggily making up his mind to crawl into his bunk and take another sleep. He still meant to have it out with Mart, but he did not feel like tackling the job just now.

Mart turned to the door and Joe got up to follow him, with a careless glance over his shoulder at Casey, who was lifting a foot as if it weighed a great deal, and was groping with it in the air trying to locate the edge of the lower bunk. Joe laughed, but the laugh died in his throat, choked off suddenly by what he saw when Mart pulled open the door.

Casey turned suspiciously at the laugh and the sound of the door opening. He swung round and steadied himself with his back against the bunk when he saw Mart and Joe lift their hands and hold them there, palms outward, a bit higher than their heads. Something in the sight enraged Casey unreasoningly. A flick of the memory may have carried him back to the old days in the mining camps when Casey drove stage and hold-ups were frequent.

"What 'r yuh tryin' to pull on me now?" he bawled, and rushed headlong toward them, pushing them forcibly out into the open with a collision of his body against Joe. Outside, a voice harshly commanded him to throw up his hands—and it was then that Casey Ryan's Irish fighting blood boiled and bubbled over. Unconsciously he pushed his hat forward over one eye, drew back his lips in a fighting grin, stepped down off the low doorsill with a lurch that nearly sent him sprawling and went weaving belligerently toward a group of five men whose attitude was anything but conciliatory.

"Casey Ryan! I'm dogged if it ain't Casey!" exclaimed a familiar voice in the group, whereat the others looked astonished. Through his slits of swollen lids Casey glared toward the voice and recognized Barney Oakes, grinning at him with what Casey considered a Judas treachery. He saw two men step away from Joe and the boss, leaving them in handcuffs.

"Take them irons off'n my friends!" bellowed Casey as he charged. "Whadda yuh think you're doin', anyway? Take 'em off! It's Casey Ryan that's tellin' yuh, an' yuh better heed what he says, before you're tore from limb to limb!"

"B-but, Casey! This 'ere's a shurf's possy!" The voice of Barney rose in a protesting 'squawk. "I brung 'em all the way over here to your rescue! They brung a cor'ner to view your remains! Don't you know your pardner, BARNEY OAKES?

"Ah-h—I know yuh think I don't? I know yuh to a fare-yuh-well! Brung a cor'ner, did yuh? Tha's all right—goin' t' need a cor'ner-but he won't set on Casey Ryan's remains—you c'n ask anybody if any cor'ners ever set on Casey Ryan yit! Naw." Casey snarled as contemptuously as was possible to a man in his condition. "No cor'ner ever set on Casey Ryan, an' he ain't goin' to!"

The men glanced questioningly at one another. One laughed. He was a large, smooth-jowled man inclined to portliness, and his laugh vibrated his entire front contagiously so that the others grinned and took it for granted that Casey Ryan was a comedy element introduced unexpectedly where they had thought to find him a tragedy.

"No, you're a pretty lively man for me to sit on; I admit it," the portly man remarked. "I'm the coroner, and it looks as if I wouldn't sit, this trip."

Casey eyed him blearily, not in the least mollified but instead swinging to a certain degree of lucidity that was nevertheless governed largely by the hoot he had swallowed in the hootch.

"There's part of a burro 'round here some'er's you c'n set on," Casey informed him grimly, and fumbled in his coat pocket for his pipe. He drew it out empty, looked at it and returned it to his pocket. One who knew Casey intimately would have detected a hidden purpose in his manner. The warning was faint, indefinable at best, and difficult to picture in words. One might say that an intimate acquaintance would have detected a false note in Casey's defiance. His manner was restrained just when violence would have been more natural.

"Damn a pipe," Casey grumbled with drunken petulance. "Anybody got a cigarette? I'm single-handed an' I ain't able t' roll 'em."

It was the coroner himself who handed Casey a "tailor-made." Casey nodded glumly, accepted a match and lighted the cigarette almost as if he were sober. He looked the group over noncommittally, eyed again the handcuffs on Mart and Joe, sent a veiled glance toward Barney Oakes and turned away. He still held the center of the stage. Fully expecting to find him dead, the sheriff and his men were slow to adjust themselves to the fact that he was very much alive and very drunk and apparently not greatly interested in his rescue.

Casey halted in his unsteady progress toward the dugout. The sheriff was already questioning his two prisoners about other members of the gang; but he looked up when Casey lifted up his voice and spoke his mind of the moment.

"Brung a cor'ner, did yuh, lookin' for some one to set on! Barney Oakes is the man that'll need a cor'ner in a minute. You're all goin' to need 'im. Casey Ryan never stood around yit whilst his friends was hobbled up by a shurf—turn 'em loose an' turn 'em loose quick! An' git back away from Barney Oakes so he won't drop on yuh in chunks—I'll fix 'im for yuh to set on!"

His hand had gone up to his cigarette, but only Joe knew what was likely to follow. Joe gave a yell of warning, ducked and ran straight away from the group. The sheriff yelled also and gave chase. The group was broken—luckily —just as Casey heaved something in that direction.

"I blowed up a jackass yesterday when they thought I couldn't—I'll blow up a bunch of 'em to-day! Yuh c'n set on what's left uh Barney Oakes!"

The explosion scattered dirt and small stones—and the sheriff's posse. Casey sent one malevolent glance over his shoulder as he stumbled into the dugout.

"Missed 'im!" he grumbled disgustedly to himself when he saw no fragments of Barney falling. His ferociousness, like the dynamite, annihilated itself with the explosion. "Missed 'im! Casey Ryan's gittin' old; old an' sick an' a damn' fool. Missed 'im with the last shot—drunk—drunk an' don't give a darn!"

He slammed the door shut behind him, pushed his hat forward so violently that it rested on the bridge of his nose, and wabbled over to his bunk. This time his foot found the edge of the lower bunk, and he scratched and clawed his way up and rolled in upon the blankets.

He was asleep and snoring when the sheriff, edging his way in as if he were an animal trainer's apprentice entering the lion's cage, sneaked on his toes to the bunk and slipped the handcuffs on Casey.

CHAPTER SEVEN

Casey awoke almost sober and considerably surprised when he discovered the handcuffs. His injured hand was throbbing from the poison in his system and the steel band on his swollen wrist. His head still ached frightfully and his tongue felt thick and dry as flannel in his mouth.

He rolled over and sat up, staring uncomprehendingly at the cabin full of men. The sight of Barney Oakes recalled in a measure his performance with the dynamite; at least, he felt a keen disappointment that Barney was alive and whole and grinning. Casey could not see what there was to grin about, and he took it as a direct insult to himself.

Mart and Joe sat sullenly on a bench against the wall, and Paw reclined in his bunk at the farther end of the room. A blood-stained bandage wrapped Paw's head turbanwise, and his little, deep-set eyes gleamed wickedly in his pallid face. Casey looked for Hank, but he was not there.

A strange man was cooking supper, and Casey wanted to tell him that he was slicing the bacon twice as thick as it should be. The corpulent man, whom he dimly remembered as a coroner, was talking with a big, burly individual whom Casey guessed was the sheriff. A man came in and announced to the big man that the car was fixed and they could go any time. Mart, who had been staring morosely down at his shackled wrists, lifted his head and spoke to the sheriff.

"You'll have to do something about my mother," he said, and bit his lip at the manner in which every head swung his way.

"What about your mother?" the sheriff asked moving toward him. "Is she here?" His eyes sent a quick glance around the room which obviously had four outside walls.

Mart swallowed. "She has a cabin to herself," he explained constrainedly. "She —she isn't quite right. Strangers excite her. She—hasn't been well since my father was killed in the mine; she's quiet enough with us—she knows us. I don't know how she'll be now. I'm afraid—but she can't be left here alone; all I ask is, be as gentle as you can."

The sheriff looked from him to Joe. Joe nodded confirmation. "Plumb harmless," he said gruffly. "It IS kinda—pitiful. Thinks everybody in the world is damned and going to hell on a long lope." He gave a snort that resembled neither mirth nor disgust. "Mebbe she's right at that," he added grimly.

The sheriff asked more questions, and Mart stood up. "I'll show you where she is, sure. But can't you leave her be till we're ready to start? She—it ain't right to bring her here."

"She'll want her supper," the sheriff reminded Mart. "We'll be driving all night. Is she sick abed?"

Casey lay down again and turned his face to the wall. He remembered the old woman now, and he hoped sincerely they would not bring her into the cabin. But whatever they did, Casey wanted no part in it whatever. He wanted to be left alone, and he wanted to think. More than all else he wanted not to see again the old woman who chanted horrible things while she rocked and rocked.

He was roused from uneasy slumber by two officious souls, one of whom was Barney Oakes. Their intentions were kindly enough, they only wanted to give him his supper. But Casey wanted neither supper nor kindly intentions, and he was still unregenerately regretful that Barney Oakes was not lying out on the garbage heap in a more or less fragmentary condition. They raised him to a sitting posture, and Casey swung his legs over the edge of the bunk and delivered a ferocious kick at Barney Oakes.

He caught Barney under the chin, and Barney went down for several counts. After that Casey wore hobbles on his feet, and was secretly rather proud of the fact that they considered him so dangerous as all that. Had his mood not been a sulky one which refused to have speech with any one there, they would probably have found it wise to gag him as well.

That is one night in Casey's turbulent life which he never recalled if he could help it. Two cars had brought the sheriff's party, and one was a seven-passenger. In the roomy rear seat of this car, Casey, shackled and savage, was made to ride with Mart and his mother. Two deputies occupied the folding seats and never relaxed their watchfulness.

Casey's head still ached splittingly, and the jolting of the car did not serve to ease the pain. The old woman sat in the middle, with a blanket wound round and round her to hold her quiet; which it failed to do. Into Casey's ear rolled the full volume of her rich contralto voice as she monotonously intoned the doom of all mankind—together with every cat, every rat, etc. Mart's fear had proved well-founded. Strangers had excited the woman and it was not until sheer exhaustion silenced her that she ceased for one moment her horrible chant.

I read the story in the morning paper, and made a flying trip to San Bernardino. Casey was in jail, naturally; but he didn't care much about that so long as he owned a head with an air-drill going inside. At least, that is what he told me when I was let in to see him. I was working to get him out of there on bail if possible before I sent word to the Little Woman, hoping she had not read the papers. I had some trouble piecing the facts together and trying to get the straight of things before I sent word to the Little Woman. I went out and got him some medicine guaranteed, by the doctor who wrote the prescription, to take the hoot out of the hootch Casey had swallowed. That afternoon Casey left off glaring at me, sat up, accepted a cigarette and consented to talk.

"—an' all I got to say is, Barney Oakes is a liar an' the father uh liars. I never was in cahoots with him at no time. When he says I got 'im to foller a Joshuay palm jest to git 'im out in the hills an' kill 'im off, he lies. Let 'im come an' tell me that there story!"

Casey was still slightly abnormal, I noticed, so I calmed him as best I could and left him alone for a time. There was some hesitancy about the bail, too, which I wished to overcome. Throwing that half-stick of dynamite might be construed as an attempt at wholesale murder. I did not want the county officials to think too long and harshly about the matter.

I explained later to Casey that Barney Oakes had reported his disappearance to the officials in Barstow. The sheriff's office had long suspected a nest of moonshiners somewhere near Black Butte, and it was rumored that one Mart Hanson, who owned a mine up there, was banking more money than was reasonable, these hard times, for a miner, who ships no ore. Casey's disappearance had crystallized the suspicions into an immediate investigation. And Barney's assertion that Casey had been murdered took the coroner along with the posse.

It had all been straight and fairly simple until they reached the mine and discovered Casey uproariously one of the gang. Throwing loaded dynamite at sheriffs is frowned upon nowadays in the best official circles, I told Casey; he would have to explain that in court, I was afraid.

Then Barney, after Casey had kicked him in the chin, had reversed his first report of the trouble and was now declaiming to all who would listen that he had been decoyed to Black Butte by Casey Ryan and there ambushed and nearly killed. Casey, as Barney now interpreted the incident, had joined his confederates under the very thin pretense of climbing the butte to come at them from behind. Barney now remembered that he had been shot at from three different angles, and that the burros had been killed by pistol shots fired at close range—presumably by Casey Ryan.

It was like taming tigers to make Casey sit still and listen to all this, but I had to do it so that he would know what to disprove. Afterwards I had a talk with Joe and Paw, separately, and so got at the whole truth. They bore no malice toward Casey and were perfectly willing to see him out of the scrape. They were a sobered pair; Hank, like a fool, had fired at the posse and was killed.

The next day came the Little Woman to the rescue. I told her the whole story, not even omitting the burro, before she went to the jail to see Casey. It was a pretty mess—take it all around—and I was secretly somewhat doubtful of the outcome.

The Little Woman is game as women are made. She went with me to the jail, and she met Casey with a whimsical smile. We found him sitting on the side of his bunk with his legs stretched out and his feet crossed, his good hand thrust in his trousers pocket and a cigarette in one corner of his mouth, which turned sourly downward. He cocked an eye up at us and rose, as the Little Woman had maybe taught him was proper. But he did not say a word until the Little Woman walked up and kissed him on both cheeks, turning his face this way and that with her hand under his chin.

Casey grinned sheepishly then and hugged her with his good arm. I wish you could have seen the look in his eyes when they dwelt on the Little Woman!

"Casey Ryan, you need a shave. And your shirt collar is a disgrace to a Piute," she drawled reprovingly.

Casey looked at me over her shoulder and grinned. He hadn't a word to say for himself, which was unusual in Casey Ryan.

"It's lucky for you, Casey Ryan, that I remembered to go down to the police station and get the proof that you were pinched twice on Broadway just five days before Barney Oakes says he found you stalled in the trail north of Barstow; and that you had been pinched pretty regularly every whip-stitch for the last six months, and were a familiar and unwelcome figure in downtown traffic and elsewhere.

"The sheriff who raided Black Butte admitted to me that it is utterly impossible for the world to hold more than one Casey Ryan at a time; and that he, for one, is willing to accept the word of the city police that you were there raising the record for traffic trouble and not moonshining at Black Butte. He doesn't approve of throwing dynamite at people, but—well, I talked with the prosecuting attorney, too, and they both seem to be mighty nice men and reasonable. I'm afraid Barney Oakes will see his beautiful story all spoiled."

"He'll forget it when he feels the ruin to his face I'm goin' t' create for him if I ever meet up with 'im again," Casey commented grimly.

"Babe sent you a pincushion she made in school. I think she made beautiful, neat stitches in that C," went on the Little Woman in a placid, gossipy tone invented especially for domestic conversation. "And—oh, yes! There's a new laundryman on our route, and he PERSISTS in running across the lawn and dumping the laundry in the front hall, though I've told him and TOLD him to deliver it at the back. And there's a new tenant in Number Six, and they hadn't been in more than three days before he came home drunk and kept everybody in the house awake, bellowing up and down the hall and abusing his wife and all. I told him held have to go when his month is up, but he says he'll be damned if he will. He says he won't and I can't make him."

"He won't, hey?" A familiar, pale glitter came into Casey's eyes. "You watch and see whether he goes or not! He better tell Casey Ryan he won't go! Who'd, they think's runnin' the place? Lemme ketch that laundry driver oncet, runnin' across our lawn; I'll run 'im across it—on his nose! They take advantage of you quick as my back's turned. I'll learn 'em they got Casey Ryan to reckon with!"

The Little Woman gave me a smiling glance over Casey's shoulder, and lowered a cautious eyelid. I left them then and went away to have a satisfying talk with the sheriff and the prosecuting attorney.

CHAPTER EIGHT

In the desert, where roads are fewer and worse than they should be, a man may travel wherever he can negotiate the rocks and sand, and none may say him nay. If any man objects, the traveler is by custom privileged to whip the objector if he is big enough, and afterwards go on his way with the full approval of public opinion. He may blaze a trail of his own, return that way a year later and find his trail an established thoroughfare.

In the desert Casey gave trail to none nor asked reprisals if he suffered most in a sudden meeting. In Los Angeles Casey was halted and rebuked on every corner, so he complained; hampered and annoyed by rules and regulations which desert dwellers never dreamed of.

Since he kept the optimistic viewpoint of a child, experience seemed to teach him little. Like the boy he was at heart, he was perfectly willing to make good resolutions—all of which were more or less theoretical and left to a kindly Providence to keep intact for him.

So here he was, after we had pried him loose from his last predicament, perfectly optimistic under his fresh haircut, and thinking the traffic cops would not remember him. Thinking, too—as he confided to the Little Woman—that Los Angeles looked pretty good, after all. He was resolved to lead henceforth a blameless life. It was time he settled down, Casey declared virtuously. His last trip into the desert was all wrong, and he wanted you to ask anybody if Casey Ryan wasn't ready at any and all times to admit his mistakes, if he ever happened to make any. He was starting in fresh now, with a new deal all around from a new deck. He had got up and walked around his chair, he told us, and had thrown the ash of a left-handed cigarette over his right shoulder; he'd show the world that Casey Ryan could and would keep out of gunshot of trouble.

He was rehearsing all this and feeling very self-righteous while he drove down West Washington Street. True, he was doing twenty-five where he shouldn't, but so far no officer had yelled at him and he hadn't so much as barked a fender. Down across Grand Avenue he larruped, never noticing the terrific bounce when he crossed the water drains there (being still fresh from desert roads). He was still doing twenty-five when he turned into Hill Street.

Busy with his good resolutions and the blameless life he was about to lead, Casey forgot to signal the left-hand turn. In the desert you don't signal, because the nearest car is probably forty or fifty miles behind you and collisions are not imminent. West-Washington-and-Hill-Street crossing is not desert, however. A car was coming behind Casey much closer than fifty miles; one of those scuttling Ford delivery trucks. It locked fenders with Casey when he swung to the left. The two cars skidded as one toward the right-hand curb; caught amidships a bright yellow, torpedo-tailed runabout coming up from Main Street, and turned it neatly on its back, its four wheels spinning helplessly in the quiet, sunny morning. Casey himself was catapulted over the runabout, landing abruptly in a sitting position on the corner of the vacant lot beyond, his self-righteousness considerably jarred.

A new traffic officer had been detailed to watch that intersection and teach a driving world that it must not cut corners. A bright, new traffic button had been placed in the geographical center of the crossing; and woe be unto the right-hand pocket of any man who failed to drive circumspectly around it. New traffic officers are apt to be keenly conscientious in their work. At twenty-five dollars per cut, sixteen unhappy drivers had been taught where the new button was located and had been informed that twelve miles per hour at that crossing would be tolerated, and that more would be expensive.

Not all drivers take their teaching meekly, and the new traffic officer near the end of his shift had pessimistically decided that the driving world is composed mostly of blamed idiots and hardened criminals.

He gritted his teeth ominously when Casey Ryan came down upon the crossing at double the legal speed. He held his breath for an instant during the crash that resounded for blocks. When the dust had settled, he ran over and yanked off the dented sand of the vacant lot a dazed and hardened malefactor who had committed three traffic crimes in three seconds: he had exceeded the speed limit outrageously, cut fifteen feet inside the red button, and failed to signal the turn.

"You damned, drunken boob!" shouted the new traffic cop and shook Casey Ryan (not knowing him).

Shaking Casey will never be safe until he is in his coffin with a lily in his hand. He was considerably jolted, but he managed a fourth crime in the next five minutes. He licked the traffic cop rather thoroughly—I suppose because his onslaught was wholly unexpected—kicked an expostulating minister in the pit of the stomach, and was profanely volunteering to lick the whole darned town when he was finally overwhelmed by numbers and captured alive; which speaks well for the L. A. P.

Wherefore Casey Ryan continued his ride down town in a dark car that wears a clamoring bell the size of a breakfast plate under the driver's foot, and a dark red L. A. Police Patrol sign painted on the sides. Two uniformed, stern-lipped cops rode with him and didn't seem to care if Casey's nose WAS bleeding all over his vest. A uniformed cop stood on the steps behind, and another rode beside the driver and kept his eye peeled over his shoulder, thinking he would be justified in shooting if anything started inside. Boys on bicycles pedaled furiously to keep up, and many an automobile barely escaped the curb because the driver was goggling at the mussed-up prisoner in the "Black Maria."

The Little Woman telegraphed me at San Francisco that night. The wire was brief but disquieting. It merely said, "CASEY IN JAIL SERIOUS NEED HELP." But I caught the Lark an hour later and thanked God it was running on time.

The Little Woman and I spent two frantic days getting Casey out of jail. The traffic cop's defeat had been rather public; and just as soon as he could stand up straight in the pulpit, the minister meant to preach a series of sermons against the laxity of a police force that permits such outrages to occur in broad daylight. More than that, the thing was in the papers, and people were reading and giggling on the street cars and in restaurants. Wherefore, the L. A. P. was on its tin ear.

Even so, much may be accomplished for a man so wholesomely human as Casey Ryan. On the third day the charge against him was changed from something worse to "Reckless driving and disturbing the peace." Casey was persuaded to plead guilty to that charge, which was harder to accomplish than mollifying the L. A. P.

He paid two fifty-dollar fines and was forbidden to drive a car "in the County of Los Angeles, State of California, during the next succeeding period of two years." He was further advised (unofficially but nevertheless with complete sincerity) to pay all damages to the two cars he had wrecked and to ask the minister's doctor what was his fee; a new uniform for the traffic cop was also suggested, since Casey had thrust his foot violently into the cop's pocket which was not tailored to resist the strain. The judge also observed, in the course of the conversation, that desert air was peculiarly invigorating and that Casey should not jeopardize his health and well-being by filling his lungs with city smoke.

I couldn't blame Casey much for the mood he was in after a setback like that to his good resolutions. I was inclined to believe with Casey that Providence had lain down on the job.

CHAPTER NINE

At the corner of the Plaza where traffic is heaviest, a dingy Ford loaded with camp outfit stalled on the street-car track just as the traffic officer spread-eagled his arms and turned with majestic deliberation to let the East-and-West traffic through. The motorman slid open his window and shouted insults at the driver, and the traffic cop left his little platform and strode heavily toward the Ford, pulling his book out of his pocket with the mechanical motion born of the grief of many drivers.

Casey Ryan, clinging to the front step of the street car on his way to the apartment house he once more called home, swung off and beat the traffic officer to the Ford. He stooped and gave a heave on the crank, obeyed a motion of the driver's head when the car started, and stepped upon the running board. The traffic officer paused, waved his book warningly and said something. The motorman drew in his head, clanged the bell, and the afternoon traffic proceeded to untangle.

"Get in, old-timer," invited the driver whom Casey had assisted. Casey did not ask whether the driver was going in his direction, but got in chuckling at the small triumph over his enemies, the police.

"Fords are mean cusses," he observed sympathetically. "They like nothing better than to get a feller in bad. But they can't pull nothin' on me. I know 'em to a fare-you-well. Notice how this one changed 'er mind about gettin' you tagged, soon as Casey Ryan took 'er by the nose?"

"Are you Casey Ryan?" The driver took his eyes off the traffic long enough to give Casey an appraising look that measured him mentally and physically. "Say, I've heard quite a lot about you. Bill Masters, up at Lund, has spoke of you often. He knows you, don't he?"

"Bill Masters sure had ought t' know me," Casey grinned. In a big, roaring, unfriendly city, here sounded a friendly, familiar tone; a voice straight from the desert, as it were. Casey forgot what had happened when Barney Oakes crossed his path claiming acquaintance with Bill Masters, of Lund. He bit off a chew of tobacco, hunched down lower in the seat, and prepared himself for a real conflab with the man who spoke the language of his tribe.

He forgot that he had just bought tickets to that evening's performance at the Orpheum, as a sort of farewell offering to his domestic goddess before once more going into voluntary exile as advised by the judge. Pasadena Avenue heard conversational fragments such as, "Say! Do you know—? Was you in Lund when—?"

Casey's new friend drove as fast as the law permitted. He talked of many places and men familiar to Casey, who was in a mood that hungered for those places and men in a spiritual revulsion against the city and all its ways.

Pasadena, Lamanda Park, Monrovia—it was not until the car slowed for the Glendora speed-limit sign that Casey lifted himself off his shoulder blades, and awoke to the fact that he was some distance from home and that the shadows were growing rather long.

"Say! I better get out here and 'phone to the missus," he exclaimed suddenly. "Pull up at a drug store or some place, will yuh? I got to talkin' an' forgot I was on my way home when I throwed in with yuh."

"Aw, you can 'phone any time. There is street cars running back to town all the time I or you can catch a bus anywhere's along here. I got pinched once for drivin' through here without a tail-light; and twice I've had blowouts right along here. This town's a jinx for me and I want to slip it behind me."

Casey nodded appreciatively. "Every darn' town's a jinx for me," he confided resentfully. "Towns an' Casey Ryan don't agree. Towns is harder on me than sour beans."

"Yeah—I guess L. A.'s a jinx for you all right. I heard about your latest run-in with the cops. I wish t' heck you'd of cleaned up a few for me. I love them saps the way I like rat poison. I've got no use for the clowns nor for towns that actually hands 'em good jack for dealin' misery to us guys. The bird never lived that got a square deal from 'em. They grab yuh and dust yuh off—"

"They won't grab Casey Ryan no more. Why, lemme tell yuh what they done!"

Glendora slipped behind and was forgotten while Casey told the story of his wrongs. In no particular, according to his version, had he been other than law-abiding. Nobody, he declaimed heatedly, had ever taken HIM by the scruff of the neck and shaken him like a pup, and got away with it, and nobody ever would. Casey was Irish and his father had been Irish, and the Ryan never lived that took sass and said thank-yuh.

His new friend listened with just that degree of sympathy which encourages the unburdening of the soul. When Casey next awoke to the fact that he was getting farther and farther away from home, they were away past Claremont and still going to the full extent of the speed limit. His friend had switched on the lights.

"I GOT to telephone my wife!" Casey exclaimed uneasily. "I'll gamble she's down to the police station right now, lookin' for me. An' I want the cops t' kinda forgit about me. I got to talkin' along an' plumb forgot I wasn't headed home."

"Aw, you can 'phone from Fontana. I'll have to stop there anyway for gas. Say, why don't yuh stall 'er off till morning? You couldn't get home for supper now if yuh went by wireless. I guess yuh wouldn't hate a mouthful of desert air after swallowing smoke and insults, like yuh done in L. A. Tell her you're takin' a ride to Barstow. You can catch a train out of there and be home to breakfast, easy. If you ain't got the change in your clothes for carfare," he added generously, "Why, I'll stake yuh just for your company on the trip. Whadda yuh say?"

Casey looked at the orange and the grapefruit and lemon orchards that walled the Foothill Boulevard. All trees looked alike to Casey, and these reminded him disagreeably of the fruit stalls in Los Angeles.

"Well, mebby I might go on to Barstow. Too late now to take the missus to the show, anyway. I guess I can dig up the price uh carfare from Barstow back." He chuckled with a sinful pride in his prosperity, which was still new enough to be novel. "Yuh don't catch Casey Ryan goin' around no more without a dime in his hind pocket. I've felt the lack of 'em too many times when they was needed. Casey Ryan's going to carry a jingle louder'n a lead burro from now on. You can ask anybody."

"You bet it's wise for a feller to go heeled," the friend of Bill Masters responded easily. "You never know when yuh might need it. Well, there's a Bell sign over there. You can be askin' your wife's consent while I gas up."

Innocent pleasure; the blameless joy of riding in a Ford toward the desert, with a prince of a fellow for company, was not so easily made to sound logical and a perfectly commonplace incident over a long-distance telephone. The Little Woman seemed struck with a sense of the unusual; her voice betrayed trepidation and she asked questions which Casey found it difficult to answer. That he was merely riding as far as Barstow with a desert acquaintance and would catch the first train back, she apparently failed to find convincing.

"Casey Ryan, tell me the truth. If you're in a scrape again, you know perfectly well that Jack and I will have to come and get you out of it. San Bernardino sounds bad to me, Casey, and you're pretty close to the place. Do you really want me to believe that you're coming back on the next train?"

"Sure as I'm standin' here! What makes yuh think I'm in a scrape? Didn't I tell yuh I'm goin' to walk around trouble from now on? When Casey tells you a thing like that, yuh got a right to put it down for the truth. I'm going to Barstow for a breath uh fresh air. This is a feller that knows Bill Masters. I'll be home to breakfast. I ain't in no trouble an' I ain't goin' to be. You can believe that or you can set there callin' Casey Ryan a liar till I git back. G'by."

Whatever the Little Woman thought of it, Casey really meant to do exactly what he said he would do. And he really did not believe that trouble was within a hundred miles of him.

CHAPTER TEN

"Wanta drive?" Casey's friend was rolling a smoke before he cranked up. "They tell me up in Lund that no man livin' ever got the chance to look back and see Casey Ryan swallowing dust. I've heard of some that's tried. But I reckon," he added pensively, while he rubbed the damp edge of the paper down carefully with a yellowed thumb, "Fords is out of your line, now. Maybe you don't toy with nothin' cheaper than a twin-six."

"Well, you can ask anybody if Casey Ryan's the man to git big-headed! Money don't spoil ME none. There ain't anybody c'n say it does. Casey Ryan is Casey Ryan wherever an' whenever yuh meet up with him. Yuh might mebby see me next, hazin' a burro over a ridge. Or yuh might see me with ten pounds uh flour, a quart uh beans an' a sour-dough bucket on my back. Whichever way the game breaks—you'll be seein' Casey Ryan; an' you'll see 'im settin' in the game an' ready t' push his last white chip to the center."

"I believe it, Casey. Darned if I don't. Well, you drive 'er awhile; till yuh get tired, anyway." He bent to the crank, gave a heave and climbed in, with Casey behind the wheel, looking pleased to be there and quite ready to show the world he could drive.

"Say, if I drive till I'm TIRED," he retorted, "I'm liable to soak 'er hubs in the Atlantic Ocean before I quit. And then, mebby I'll back 'er out an' drive 'er to the end of Venice Pier just for pastime."

"Up in Lund they're talkin' yet about your drivin'," his new friend flattered him. "They say there's no stops when you get the wheel cuddled up to your chest. No quittin' an' no passin' yuh by with a merry laugh an' a cloud of alkali dust. I guess it's right. I've been wantin' to meet yuh."

"That there last remark sounds like a traffic cop I had a run-in with once!" Casey snorted—merely to hide his gratification. "You sound good, just to listen to, but you ain't altogether believable. There's men in Lund that'd give an ear to meet me in a narrow trail with a hairpin turn an' me on the outside an' drunk.

"They'd like it to be about a four-thousand-foot drop, straight down. Lund as a town ain't so crazy about me that they'd close up whilst I was bein' planted, an' stop all traffic for five minutes. A show benefit was sprung on Lund once, to help Casey Ryan that was supposed to be crippled. An' I had to give a good Ford—a DARN' good Ford!—to the benefitters, so is they could git outa town ahead uh the howlin' mob. That's how I know the way Lund loves Casey Ryan. Yuh can't kid ME, young feller."

Meanwhile, Casey swung north into Cajon Pass; up that long, straight, cement-paved highway to the hills he showed his new friend how a Ford could travel when Casey Ryan juggled the wheel. The full moon was pushing up into a cloud bank over a high peak beyond the Pass. The few cars they met were gone with a whistle of wind as Casey shot by.

He raced a passenger train from the mile whistling-post to the crossing, made the turn and crossed the track with the white finger of the headlight bathing the Ford blindingly. He completed that S turn and beat the train to the next crossing half a mile farther on; where he "spiked 'er tail", as he called it, stopping dead still and waiting jeeringly for the train to pass. The engineer leaned far out of the cab window to bellow his opinion of such driving; which was unfavorable to the full extent of his vocabulary.

"Nothin' the matter with a Ford, as I can see," Casey observed carelessly, when he was under way again.

"You sure are some driver," his new friend praised him, letting go the edge of the car and easing down again into the seat. "Give yuh a Ford and all the gas yuh can burn and I can't see that you'd need to worry none about any of them saps that makes it their business to interfere with travelin'. I'm glad that moon's quit the job. Gives the headlights a show. Hit 'er up now, fast as yuh like. After that crossin' back there I ain't expectin' to tremble on no curves. I see you're qualified to spin 'er on a plate if need be. And for a Ford, she sure can travel."

Casey therefore "let 'er out", and the Ford went like a scared lizard up the winding highway through the Pass. At Cajon Camp he slowed, thinking they would need to fill the radiator before attempting to climb the steep grade to the summit. But the young man shook his head and gave the "highball." (Which, if you don't already know it, is the signal for full speed ahead.)

Full speed ahead Casey gave him, and they roared on up the steep, twisting grade to the summit of the Pass. Casey began to feel a distinct admiration for this particular Ford. The car was heavily loaded—he could gauge the weight by the "feel" of the car as he drove yet it made the grade at twenty-five miles an hour and reached the top without boiling the radiator; which is better than many a more pretentious car could do.

"Too bad you've made your pile already," the young man broke a long silence. "I'd like to have a guy like you for my pardner. The desert ain't talkative none when you're out in the middle of it, and you know there ain't another human in a day's drive. I've been going it alone. Nine-tenths of these birds that are eager to throw in with yuh thinks that fifty-fifty means you do the work and they take the jack. I'm plumb fed upon them pardnerships. But if you didn't have your jack stored away—a hull mountain of it, I reckon—I'd invite yuh to set into the game with me; I sure would."

Casey spat into the dark beside the car. "They's never a pile so big a feller ain't willin' to make it bigger," he replied sententiously. "Fer, as I'm concerned, Casey's never backed up from a dollar yet. But I ain't no wild colt no more, runnin' loose an' never a halter mark on me. I'm bein' broke to harness, and it's stable an' corral from now on, an' no more open range fer Casey. The missus hopes to high-school me in time. She's a good hand—gentle but firm, as the preacher says. And I guess it's time fer Casey Ryan to quit hellin' around the country an' settle down an' behave himself."

"I could put you in the way of adding some easy money to your bank roll," the other suggested tentatively.

But Casey shook his head. "Twenty years ago yuh needn't have asked me twice, young feller. I'd 'a' drawed my chair right up and stacked my chips a mile high. Any game that come along, I played 'er down to the last chip. Twenty years ago—yes, er ten!—Casey Ryan woulda tore that L. A. jail down rock by rock an' give the roof t' the kids to make a playhouse. Them L. A. cops never woulda hauled me t' jail in no wagon. I mighta loaded 'em in behind, and dropped 'em off at the first morgue an' drove on a-whistlin'. That there woulda been Casey Ryan's gait a few years back. Take me now, married to a good woman an' gettin' gray—" Casey sighed, gazing wishfully back at the Casey Ryan he had been and might never be again.

"No, sir, I ain't so darned rich I ain't willin' to add a few more iron men to the bunch. But on account of the missus I've got to kinda pick my chances. I ain't had money so long but what it feels good to remind myself I got it. I carry a thousand dollars or so in my inside pocket, just to count over now an' then to convince myself I needn't worry about a grubstake. I've got to soak it into my bones gradual that I can afford to settle down and live tame, like the missus wants. Stand-up collars every day, an' step into a chiny bathtub every night an' scrub—when you ain't doin' nothin' to git dirt under your finger nails even! Funny, the way city folks act. The less they do to git dirty, the more soap they wear out. You can ask anybody if that ain't right.

"Can't chew tobacco in the house, even, 'cause there's no place yuh dast to spit. I stuck m' head out of the bedroom window oncet, an I let fly an' it landed on a lady; an' the missus went an' bought her a new hat an took my plug away from me. I had to keep my chewin' tobacco in the tool-box of my car, after that, an' sneak out to the beach now an' then an' chew where I could spit in the ocean. That's city life for yuh!"

"When I git to thinkin' about hittin' out into the hills prospectin, or somethin', that roll uh dough I pack stands right on its hind legs an' says I got no excuse. I've got enough to keep me in bacon an' beans, anyway. An' the missus gits down in the mouth when I so much as mention minin'."

"A guy grows old fast when he quits the game and sets down to do the grandpa-by-the-fire. First you know, a clown that thinks it's time he took it easy is gummin' 'is grub, and shiverin' when yuh open the door, an' takin' naps in the daytime same as babies. Let a guy once preach he's gettin' old—"

Casey jerked the gas lever and jumped the car ahead viciously. "Well, now, any time yuh see CASEY RYAN gummin' 'is grub an' needin' a nap after dinner—"

"A clown GITS that way once he pulls out of the game. I've saw it happen time an' again." The young man laughed rather irritatingly. "Say, when I tell it to Bill Masters that Casey Ryan has plumb played out his string an' laid down an' QUIT, by hock, and can be seen hereafter SETTIN' WITH A SHAWL OVER HIS SHOULDERS—"

Casey nearly turned the Ford over at that insult. He jerked it back into the road and sent it ahead again at a faster pace.

"Well, now, any time yuh see CASEY RYAN settin' with a shawl over his shoulders—"

"Well, maybe not YOU; but the bird sure comes to it that thinks he's too old to play the game. Why, you'll never be ready to settle down! Take yuh twenty years from now—I'd rather bank on a pardner like you'd be than some young clown that ain't had the experience. From the yarns I've heard about yuh, yuh don't back down from nothing. And you're willing to give a pardner a chance to get away with his hide on him. I'd rather be held up by the law than by some clown that's workin' with me."

He paused; and when he, spoke again his tone had changed to meet a prosaic detail of the drive.

"Stop here in Victorville, will yuh, Casey? I'll take a look at the radiator and maybe take on some more gas and oil. I've been stuck on the desert a few times with an empty tank—and that learns a guy to keep the top of his gas tank full and never mind the bottom."

"Good idea," said Casey shortly, his own tone relaxing its tension of a few minutes before. "I run a garage over at Patmos once, an' the boobs I seen creepin' in on their last spoonful uh gas—walkin' sometimes for miles to carry gas back to where they was stalled—learnt Casey Ryan to fill 'er up every chancet he gits."

But although the subject of age had been dropped half a mile back in the sand, certain phrases flung at him had been barbed and had bitten deep into Casey Ryan's self-esteem. They stung and rankled there. He had squirmed at the picture his new friend had so ruthlessly drawn with crude words, but bold, of doddering old age. Casey resented the implication that he might one day fill that picture.

He began vaguely to resent the Little Woman's air of needing to protect him from himself. Casey Ryan, he told himself boastfully, had never needed protection from anybody. He had managed for a good many years to get along on his own hook. The Little Woman was all right, but she was making a mistake—a big mistake—if she thought she had to close-herd him to keep him out of trouble.

He rolled a smoke and wished that the Little Woman would settle down with him somewhere in the desert, where he could keep a couple of burros and go prospecting in the hills. Where sagebrush could grow to their very door if it wanted to, and the moon could show them long stretches of mesa land shadowed with mystery, and then drop out of sight behind high peaks.

He felt that he might indeed grow old fast, shut up in a city. It occurred to him that the Little Woman was unreasonable to expect it of him. Her idea of getting him out of town for a time, as the judge had advised, was to send him up to San Francisco to be close-herded there. Casey had promised to go, but now the prospect jarred. He wasn't feeble-minded, that he knew of; it seemed natural to want to do his own deciding now and then. When he got back home in the morning, Casey meant to have a serious talk with the Little Woman, and get right down to cases, and tell her that he was built for the desert, and that you can't teach an old dog new tricks.

"They been tryin' to make Casey Ryan over into something he ain't," he muttered under his breath, while his new friend was in the garage office paying for the gas. "Jack an' the Little Woman's all right, but they can't drive Casey Ryan in no town herd. Cops is cops; and they got 'em in San Francisco same as they got 'em in L. A. If they got 'em, I'll run agin' 'em. I'll tell 'em so, too."

The young man came out, sliding silver coins into his trousers pocket. He glanced up and down the narrow, little street already deserted, cranked the Ford and climbed in.

"All set," he observed cheerfully, "Let's go!"

Casey slipped his cigarette to the upper, left-hand corner of his whimsical, Irish mouth, forced a roar out of the little engine and whipped around the corner and across the track into the faintly lighted road that led past shady groves and over a hill or two, and so into the desert again.

His new friend had fallen into a meditative mood, staring out through the windshield and whistling under his breath a pleasant little melody of which he was probably wholly unaware. Perhaps he felt that he had said enough to Casey just at present concerning a possible partnership. Perhaps he even regretted having said anything at all.

Casey himself drove mechanically, his rebellious mood slipping gradually into optimism. You can't keep Casey Ryan down for long; in spite of his past unpleasant experiences he was presently weaving optimistic plans of his own. The young fellow beside him seemed to return Casey's impulsive friendship. Casey thought pleasureably of the possibility of their driving over the desert together, sharing alike the fortunes of the game and the adventures of the trail. Casey himself had learned to be shy of partnerships—witness Barney Oakes! —but any man with a drop of Irish in his blood and a bit of Irish twinkle in his eye would turn his back on defeat and try again for a winning.

They had just passed over a hilly stretch with many turns and windings, the moon blotted out completely now by the cloud bank. For half an hour they had not seen any evidence that other human beings were alive in the world. But when they went rattling across a small mesa where the sand was deep, a car with one brilliant spotlight suddenly showed itself around a turn just ahead of them.

Casey slowed down automatically and gave a twist to the steering wheel. But the sand just here was deep and loose, and the front wheels of the Ford gouged unavailingly at the sides of the ruts. Casey honked the horn warningly and stopped full, swearing a good, Caseyish oath. The other car, having made no apparent effort to turn out, also stopped within a few feet of Casey, the spotlight fairly blinding him.

The young man beside Casey slid up straight in the seat and stopped whistling. He leaned out of the car and stared ahead without the dusty interference of the windshield.

"You can back up a few lengths and make the turn-out all right," he suggested.

"If I can back up, so can he. He's got as much road behind him as what I'VE got," Casey retorted stubbornly. "He never made a try at turnin' out. I was watchin'. Any time I can't lick a road hawg, he's got a license to lick me. Make yourself comf'table, young feller—we're liable to set here a spell." Casey grinned. "I spent four hours on a hill once, out-settin, a road hawg that wanted me to back up."

The man in the other car climbed out and came toward them, walking outside the beams cast by his own glaring spotlight. He bulked rather large in the shadows; but Casey Ryan, blinking at him through the windshield, was still ready and willing to fight if necessary. Or, if stubbornness were to be the test, Casey could grin and feel secure. A little man, he reflected, can sit just as long as a big man.

The big man walked leisurely up to the car and smiled as he lifted a foot to the running board. He leaned forward, his eyes going past Casey to the other man.

"I kinda thought it was you, Kenner," he drawled. "How much liquor you got aboard to-night?"

Casey, slanting a glance downward, glimpsed the barrel of a big automatic looking toward them.

"What if I ain't got any?" the young man parried glumly. "You're taking a lot for granted."

The big man chuckled. "If you ain't loaded with hootch, it's because one of the boys met up with yuh before I did. Open 'er up. Lemme see what you got."

The young fellow scowled, swore under his breath and climbed out, turning toward the loaded tonneau with reluctant obedience.

"I can't argue with the law," he said, as he began to pull out a roll of bedding wedged in tightly. "But, for cripes sake, go as easy as you can. I'm plumb lame from my last fall!"

The big man chuckled again. "The law's merciful as, it can afford to be, and I've got a heart like an ox. Got any jack on yuh?"

"I'm just about cleaned, and that's the Gawd's truth. Have a heart, can't yuh? A man's got t' live."

"Slip me five hundred, anyway. How much is your load?"

"Sixty gallons—bottled, most of it. Two kegs in bulk." Young Kenner was proceeding stoically with the unloading. Casey, his mouth clamped tight shut, was glaring stupifiedly straight out through the windshield.

"Pile out thirty gallons of the bottled goods by that bush. You can keep the kegs." The big man's eyes shifted to Casey Ryan's expressionless profile and dwelt there curiously.

"Seems like I know you," he said abruptly. "Ain't you the guy that was brought in with that Black Butte bunch of moonshiners and got off on account of a nice wife and an L. A. alibi? Sure you are! Casey Ryan. I got yuh placed now." He threw back his head and laughed.

Casey might have been an Indian making a society call for all the sign of life he gave. Young Kenner, having deposited his camp outfit in a heap on the ground, began lifting out tall, round bottles, four at a time and ricking them neatly beside the large sagebush indicated by the officer.

Standing upon the running board at Casey's shoulder where he had a clear view, the big man watched the unloading and at the same time kept an eye on Casey. It was perfectly evident that for all his easy good nature, he was not a man who could be talked out of his purpose.

"All right, pile in your blankets," the big man ordered at last, and young Kenner unemotionally began to reload the camp outfit. The big man's attention shifted to Casey again. He looked at him curiously and grinned.

"Say, that's a good one you pulled! You had all the county officials bluffed into thinking you were the victim of that Black Butte bunch, instead of being in cahoots. That alibi of yours was a bird. Does Kenner, here, know you hit the hootch pretty strong at times? Bootlegging's bad business for a man that laps it up the way you do. Where's that piece of change, Kenner?"

"Aw, can't yuh find some way to leave me jack enough to buy gas and grub?" Young Kenner asked sullenly, reaching into his pocket. The big man shook his head.

"I'm doing a lot for you boys, when I let yuh get past me with the Lizzie, to say nothing of half your load. I'd ought to trundle yuh back to San Berdoo; you both know that as well as I do. I'm too soft-hearted for this job, anyway. Hand over the roll."

Young Kenner swore and extended his arm behind Casey. "That leaves me six bits," he growled, as the big man dropped something into his coat pocket. "You might give me back ten, anyway."

"Couldn't possibly. I have to have something to square myself with if this leaks out. Just back up, till you can get around my car. Turn to the left where the sand ain't so deep and you ain't likely to run over the booze."

With the big man still standing at his shoulder on the running board, Casey Ryan did what he had rashly declared he never would do; he backed the Ford, turned it to the left as he had been commanded to do, and drove around the other car. It was bitter work for Casey; but even he recognized the fact that the "settin'" was not good that evening. Back in the road again, he stopped when he was told to stop, and waited, with a surface calm altogether strange to Casey, while the officer stepped off and gave a bit of parting advice.

"Better keep right on going, boys. I'd hate to see yuh get in trouble, so you'd better take this old road up ahead here. That'll bring yuh out at Dagget and you'll miss Barstow altogether. I just came from there; there's a hard gang hanging around on the lookout for anything they can pick up. Don't get caught again. On your way!"

Casey drove for half a mile still staring straight before him. Then young Kenner laughed shortly.

"That's Smilin' Lou," he said. "He's a mean boy to monkey with. Talk about road hawgs—he's one yuh can't outset!"

CHAPTER ELEVEN

"So that's the kind uh game yuh asked me to set in on!" Casey broke another long silence. He had felt in his bones that young Kenner was watching him secretly, waiting for him to take his stand for or against the proposition.

"I'd like to know who passed the word around amongst outlaws that Casey Ryan is the only original easy mark left runnin' wild, an' that he can be caught an' made a goat of any time it's handy! Look at the crowd of folks bunched on that crossing this afternoon! Why didn't yuh pick some one else for the goat? Outa all them hundreds uh people, why'n hell did yuh have to go an' pick on Casey Ryan? Ain't he had trouble enough tryin' to keep outa trouble?

"Naw! Casey Ryan's went an' blowed hisself to show tickets, an' he's headed home, peaceful an' on time, so's he can shave an' put on a clean collar an' slick up to please his wife an' take 'er to the show! Nothin' agin the law in that! Not a damn' thing yuh can haul 'im to jail fer! So YOU had to come along, loaded to the guards with hootch—stall your Ford on the car track right under m' nose, an' tell Casey Ryan to git in! Couldn't leave 'im to go home peaceful to 'is wife—naw! You had t' haul 'im away out here an' git 'im in wrong with a cop agin! That's a fine game you're playin'! That's a DARNED fine game!"

"Sure, it is! It's better than the game you've been playing," young Kenner stated calmly. "Take your own story, for instance. You've been dubbin' along, tryin' t' play the way the law tells you to. An' the saps has been flockin' to yuh like a bunch uh hornets—every bird tryin' t' sink his stinger in first. Ain't that right?

"Keepin' the law has laid yuh in jail twice in the last month, by your own tell. Why, a clown like you, that's aimin' t' keep the law an' live honest, is the easiest mark in the world. Them's the guys that do the most harm—they make graftin' so darned easy! Them's the guys the saps lay for and dust off regular in the shape of fines an' taxes an' the like uh that. Oncet in awhile they'll snatch yuh fer somethin' yuh never done at all an' lay yuh away fer a day or two, just t' keep yuh scared and easy t' handle next time.

"Now, yuh take me, fer instance. I play agin' the law—an' I'm cleanin' up right along, and have yet to take my morning sunlight in streaks. I know as much about the inside of a jail as I know about the White House—an' no more. I've hauled hootch all over the country, an' I never yet was dusted off so hard by the law that I didn't come through with a roll uh jack they'd overlooked.

"Take this highjackin' to-night, for instance. Look what Smilin' Lou took off'n me! And yet," Kenner turned and grinned impudently at Casey, "don't never think I didn't come out a long jump ahead! I carry nothin' cheap; nothin' but good whisky an' brandy that the liquor houses failed to declare when the world went dry. Then there's real, honest-to-gosh European stuff run in from Mexico; now you're in, Casey, I'll tell yuh the snap. When I said easy money, I was in my right mind.

"You can count on highjackers leavin' yuh half your load; mebby a little more, if yuh set purty. They don't aim t' force yuh out uh the business. They grab what the traffic'll bear, an' let yuh go on an make a profit so you'll stay.

"Now there's a card you can slip up your sleeve for this game. Yuh load in the best stuff first—see? Anything real special you wanta put in kegs with double sides an' ends which you fill with moonshine. Yuh never can tell—they might wanta sample it. Smilin' Lou did once—an' you notice to-night he left the kegs be. So they get a good grade of whisky from the liquor houses. And they pass up the best, imported stuff that can be got to-day. We'll have regular customers for that; and you can gamble they'll pay the price!" He laughed at some secret joke which he straightway shared with Casey.

"You noticed I got my gas-tank behind—a twenty-gallon tank at that. Well, what if I tell yuh that right under this front seat there's a false bottom to the tool-box and under that—well, suppose you're settin' on forty pints uh French champagne? More'n all that, this cushion we're settin' on has got a concealed pocket down both sides—for hop. So yuh see, Casey, a man can make an honest livin' at this game, even if he's highjacked every trip. Now you're in, I can show yuh all kinds uh tricks."

The muscles, along Casey's jaw had hardened until they looked bunched. His eyes, fixed upon the winding trail in front of him, were a pale, unwinking glitter.

"Who says I'm in? Yuh ain't heard Casey Ryan say it yet, have yuh? Yuh better wait till Casey says he's in b'fore yuh bank on 'im too strong. Casey may be an easy mark—he may be the officious goat pro tem of every darn' bootlegger an' moonshiner an' every darn' cop that crosses his trail; but you can ask anybody if Casey Ryan don't do 'is own decidin'!"

"Before you go any further, young feller, I'll tell yuh just how fur Casey's in your game—an' that's as fur as Barstow. When Casey says he'll do a thing he comes purty near doin' it. I ain't playin' no bootleg game, young feller; White Mule an' me ain't an' never was trail pardners. Make me choose between bootleggers an' cops, an' I'd have to flip a dollar on it. Only fer Bill Masters bein' your friend, I dunno but what I'd take yuh right back with me t' L. A. an' let yuh sleep in a jail oncet—seein' you've never had the pleasure!"

The young man laughed imperturbably. "Flip that dollar for me, Casey, to see whether I shoot yuh now an' dump yuh out in the brush somewheres, or make yuh play the hootch game an' like it. Why, you didn't think for one minute, did yuh, that I was takin' any chance with you? Not a chance in the world! Go squeal to the law—an' what would it get yuh?

"You was drivin' this car yourself when Smilin' Lou stopped us, recollect. He had yuh placed as one of that Black Butte gang quick as he lamped yuh. Yuh think Smilin' Lou is goin' to take a chance? You was caught with the goods t'night, old-timer, an' it's the second time inside a month. It'd be the third time you an' the law has tangled. Why, you set there yourself an' told me how you was practically run outa L. A., right this week. You set still a minute and figure out about how many years they'd give yuh!

"How come Smilin' Lou overlooked cleanin' yuh of your roll when he took mine, do yuh think? He was treatin' yuh white, an' givin' yuh a chance to come back strong next time—that's why. They got so much on yuh now after to-night, that he knows you got just one chance to sidestep a stretch in the pen. That's to play the game with pertection. Smilin' Lou never to my knowledge throwed down a guy that come through on demand.

"Smilin' Lou stood there an' sized yuh up about the same as I did, somethin' like this: 'Here Is Casey Ryan—a clown that's safe anywhere in the desert States. He got honest prospector wrote all over 'im. Why, if you boarded a street car the conductor would be guessin', wild-eyed, how much gold dust it takes to make a nickel, expectin' you to haul out your poke an' look around fer the gold scales. Why, you could git by where a town guy couldn't. You've got a rep a mile long as a fightin', squareshootin' Irishman that's a drivin' fool an' knows the desert like he knows ham-an'-eggs. Tie on some picks an' shovels an' put you behind the wheel, and only the guys that are in the know would ever get wise in a thousand years.

"Why, look what he said about you havin' 'em all bluffed in San Berdoo! Grabbed you with a bunch uh moonshiners, and you fightin' the saps harder'n any of 'em—and then, by heck, you slips the noose an' leaves 'em thinkin' you're honest but unlucky.

"So you 'n' me is pardners till I say when. We'll clean up some real jack together. Minin' ain't in it, no more, with hootch runnin'—if yuh play it right. The good old White Mule goes under the wire, old-timer, an' takes the money. Burros is extinct."

"Burros ain't any extincter than what you'll be when I git through with yuh," gritted Casey savagely, shutting off the gas. "Bill Masters can like it or not— I'm goin' to lick the livin' tar outa you here an' now. When I'm through with yuh, if you're able to wiggle the wheel, yuh can take your load uh hootch an' go tahell! I'll hoof it down here to the next station on the railroad an' ketch a ride back to L. A."

Kenner laughed. "An' what would I be doin', you poor nut? Set here meek till yuh tell me to git out an' take a lickin'? Yuh feel that gun proddin' yuh in the ribs, don't yuh? I can't help wonderin' how your wife would feel towards you if you was found with a hole drilled through your middle, an' a carload uh booze. That'd jar the faith of the most believin' woman on earth. You take this cut-off road up here an' drive till I tell yuh t' stop. As you may know, a man can't be chickenhearted and peddle hootch—an' I'm called an expert. So you think that over, Casey—an' drive purty, see?"

Casey drove as "purty" as was possible with a six-shooter pressed irritatingly against his lowest floating rib; but he did not dwell upon the spectacle of himself found dead with a carload of booze. He wished to heaven he hadn't let the Little Woman talk him out of packing a gun, and waited for his chance.

Young Kenner was thoughtful, brooding through the hours of darkness with his head slightly bent and his eyes, so far as Casey could determine, fixed steadily on the uneven trail where the headlights revealed every rut, every stone, every chuck-hole. But Casey was not deceived by that quiescence. The revolver barrel never once ceased its pressure against his side, and he knew that young Kenner never for an instant forgot that he was riding with Casey Ryan at the wheel, waiting for a chance to kill him.

By daylight, such was Casey's driving, they were well down the highway which leads to Needles and on through Arizona. Casey was just thinking that they would soon run out of gas, and that he would then have a fighting chance, when he was startled almost into believing that he had spoken his plan.

"I told you there's a twenty-gallon tank on this car; well, it holds twenty-five. I've got a special carburetor that gives an actual mileage of twenty-two miles to the gallon on ordinary desert roads. I filled 'er till she run over at Victorville —and I notice you're easy on the gas with your drivin'. Figure it yourself, Casey, and don't be countin' on a stop till I'm ready t' stop."

Casey grunted, more crestfallen than he would ever admit. But he hadn't given up; the give-up quality had been completely forgotten when Casey's personality was being put together. He drove on, around the rubbly base of a blackened volcano long since cold and bleak, and bored his way through the sandy stretch that leads through Patmos.

Patmos was a place of unhappy memories, but he drove through the little hamlet so fast that he scarcely thought of his unpleasant sojourn there the summer before. Young Kenner had fallen silent again and they drove the sixty miles or so to Goffs with not a word spoken between them.

Casey spent most of that time in mentally cursing the Ford for its efficiency. He had prayed for blowouts, a fouled timer, for something or anything or everything to happen that could possibly befall a Ford. He couldn't even make the radiator boil. Worst and most persistent of his discomforts was the hard pressure of that six-shooter against his side. Casey was positive that the imprint of it would be worn as a permanent brand upon his person for the rest of his life. Young Kenner's voice speaking to him came so abruptly that Casey jumped.

"I've been thinking over your case," Kenner said cheerfully. "Stop right here while we talk it over."

Casey stopped right there.

"I've changed my mind about havin' you for a pardner," young Kenner went on. "You'd be a valuable man all right; but when a harp like you gets stubborn-bitter, my hunch tells me to break away clean. You're a mick—an' micks is all alike when they git a grudge. I can't be bothered keepin' yuh under my eye all the time, and the way I've felt yuh oozin' venom all this while shows me I'd have to. An' bumpin' yuh off would be neither pleasant ner safe.

"Now, the way I've doped this out, I'm goin' to sell yuh the outfit fer just what jack yuh got in your clothes. Fork it over, an' I'll give yuh the layout just as she stands."

"Yuh better wait till Casey says he wants t' buy!" Swallowing resentment all night had made his voice husky; and it was bitter indeed to sit still and hear himself called a harp and a mick.

"Why wait? Hand over the roll, and that closes the deal. I didn't ask yuh would yuh buy—I'm givin' yuh somethin' fer your money, is all. I could take it off yuh after yuh quit kickin' and drive your remains in to this little burg, with a tale of how I'd caught a bootlegger that resisted arrest. So fork over the jack, old-timer. I want to catch that train over there that's about ready to pull out." He prodded sharply with the gun, and Casey heard a click which needed no explanation.

Casey fumbled for a minute inside his vest and glumly "forked over." Young Kenner inspected the folded bank notes, smiled and slipped the flat bundle inside his shirt.

"You're stronger on the bank roll than what yuh let on," he remarked contentedly. "I don't stand to lose so much, after all. Sixteen hundred, I make it. What's in your pants pockets?"

Casey, still balefully silent, emptied first one pocket and then the other into Kenner's cupped palm. With heavy sarcasm he felt in his watch pocket and produced a nickel slipped there after paying street-car fare. He held it out to young Kenner between his finger and thumb, still gazing straight before him.

Young Kenner took it and grinned. "Oh, well—you're rich! Drive on now, and when you get about even with that caboose, slow to twelve miles whilst I hop off; and then hit 'er up again an' keep 'er goin'. If yuh don't, I'll grab yuh fer a bootlegger, sure. And I'd have the hull train crew to help me wrassle yuh down. They'd be willin' to sample the evidence, I guess, an' be witnesses against yuh. An' bear in mind, Casey, that yuh got a darned good Ford and all its valuable contents for sixteen hundred and some odd bucks. If you meet up with the law, you can treat 'em white an' still break even on the deal yuh just consummated with me."

"Like hell I consummated the deal!" Casey was goaded into muttering.

He drove abreast of the caboose, and at a final prod in the ribs Casey slowed down. Young Kenner dropped off the running board, alighted running with his body slanted backwards and his lips smiling friendly-wise.

"Don't take any bad money—an' don't let 'em catch yuh!" he cried mockingly, as he headed for the caboose.

At a crossing, two miles farther on, Casey came larruping out of the sand hills and was forced to wait while the freight train went rattling past, headed east on a downhill grade.

Young Kenner, up in the cupola, leaned far out and waved his hat as the caboose flicked by.

CHAPTER TWELVE

The highway north from the Santa Fe Railroad just west of Needles climbs an imperceptible grade across barren land to where the mesa changes and becomes potentially fertile. Up this road, going north, a cloud of yellow dust rolled swiftly. See at close range, the nose of a dingy Ford protruded slightly in front of the enveloping cloud—and behind it Casey Ryan, hard-eyed and with his jaw set to the fighting mood, gripped the wheel and drove as if he had a grudge against the road.

At the first signpost Casey canted a malevolent eye upward and went lurching by at top speed. The car bulked black for a moment, dimmed, and merged into the fleeing cloud that presently seemed no more than a dust-devil whirling across the mesa. At the second signpost Casey slowed, his eyes dwelling speculatively upon the legend:

"JUNIPER WELLS 3 M"

The arrow pointed to the right where a narrow, little-used trail angled crookedly away through the greasewood. Casey gave a deciding twist to the steering wheel and turned into the trail.

Juniper Wells is not nearly so nice a place as it sounds. But it is the first water north of the Santa Fe, and now and then a wayfarer of the desert leaves the main highway and turns that way, driven by necessity. It is a secluded spot, too unattractive to tempt people to linger; because of its very seclusion it therefore tempted Casey Ryan.

When a man has driven a Ford fifteen hours without once leaving the wheel or taking a drink of water or a mouthful of food, however great his trouble or his haste, his first thought will be of water, food and rest. Even Casey's deadly rage at the diabolical trick played upon him could not hold his thoughts from dwelling upon bacon and coffee and a good sleep afterwards.

Wind and rain and more wind, buffeting that trail since the last car had passed, made "heavy going." The Ford labored up small hills and across gullies, dipping downward at last to Juniper Wells; there Casey stopped close beside the blackened embers left by some forgotten traveler of the wild. He slid stiffly from behind the wheel to the vacant seat beside him, and climbed out like the old man he had last night determined never to become. He walked away a few paces, turned and stood glaring back at the car as if familiarizing himself with an object little known and hated much.

Fate, he felt, had played a shabby trick upon an honest man. Here he stood, a criminal in the eyes of the law, a liar in the eyes of the missus. An honest man and a truthful, here he was—he, Casey Ryan—actually afraid to face his fellow men.

"HE wasn't no friend of Bill Masters; the divil himself wouldn'ta owned him fer a friend!" snarled Casey, thinking of Kenner. "Me—CASEY RYAN!— with a load uh booze wished onto me—and a car that may have been stolen fer all I know—an' not a darn' nickel to my name! They can make a goat uh Casey Ryan once, but watch clost when they try it the second time! Casey MAY be gittin' old; he might possibly have softenin' of the brain; but he'll git the skunk that done this, or you'll find his carcass layin' alongside the trail bleachin' like a blowed-out tire! I'll trail 'im till my tongue hangs down to my knees! I'll git 'im an' I'll drown 'im face down in a bucket of his own booze!" Whipped by emotion, his voice rose stridently until it cracked just under a shout.

"That sounds pretty businesslike, old man," a strange voice spoke whimsically behind Casey. "Who's all this you're going to trail till your tongue hangs down to your knees? Going to need any help?"

Casey whirled belligerently upon the man who had walked quietly up behind him.

"Where the hell did YOU come from?" he countered roughly.

"Does it matter? I'm here," the other parried blandly. "But by the way! If you've got the makings of a meal in your car—and you look too old a hand in the desert to be without grub—I won't refuse to have a snack with you. I hate to invite myself to breakfast, but it's that or go hungry—and an empty belly won't stand on ceremony."

The hard-bitten features of Casey Ryan, tanned as they were by wind and sun to a fair imitation of leather, were never meant to portray mixed emotions. His face, therefore, remained impassive except for a queer, cornered look in his eyes. With a sick feeling at the pit of his stomach he wondered just how much of his impassioned soliloquy the man had overheard; who and what this man was, and how he had managed to approach within six feet of Casey without being overheard. With a sicker feeling, he wondered if there were any grub in the car; and if so, how he could get at it without revealing his contraband load to this stranger.

But Casey Ryan was nothing if not game. He reached for his trusty plug of tobacco and pried off a corner with his teeth. He lifted his left hand mechanically to the back of his head and pushed his black felt hat forward so that it rested over his right eyebrow at a devil-may-care angle. These preparations made involuntarily and unconsciously, Casey Ryan was himself again.

"All right—if you're willin' to rustle the wood an' start a fire, I'll see if I can dig up somethin'." He cocked an eye up at the sun. "I et my breakfast long enough ago so I guess it's settled. I reckon mebby I c'd take on some bacon an' coffee myself. Feller I had along with me I ditched, back here at the railroad. He done the packin' up—an' I'd hate to swear to what he put in an' what he left out. Onery cuss—I wouldn't put nothin' past him. But mebby we can make out a meal."

The stranger seemed perfectly satisfied with this arrangement and studied preamble. He started off to gather dead branches of greasewood; and Casey, having prepared the way for possible disappointment, turned toward the car.

Fear and Casey Ryan have ever been strangers; yet he was conscious of a distinct, prickly chill down his spine. The glance he cast over his shoulder at the stranger betrayed uneasiness, best he could do. He turned over the roll of bedding and cautiously began a superficial search which he hoped would reveal grub in plenty—without revealing anything else. He wished now that he had taken a look over his shoulder when young Kenner was unloading the car at Smiling Lou's command. He would be better prepared now for possible emergencies. He remembered, with a bit of comfort, that the bootlegger had piled a good deal of stuff upon the ground before Casey first heard the clink of bottles.

A grunt of relief signaled his location of a box containing grub. A moment later he lifted out a gunny sack bulging unevenly with cooking utensils. He fished a little deeper, turned back a folded tarp and laid naked to his eyes the top of a whisky keg. With a grunt of consternation he hastily replaced the tarp, his heart flopping in his chest like a fresh-landed fish.

The stranger was kneeling beside a faintly crackling little pile of twigs, his face turned inquiringly toward Casey. Casey, glancing guiltily over his shoulder, felt the chill hand of discovery reaching for his very soul. It was as if a dead man were hidden away beneath that tarp. It seemed to him that the eyes of the stranger were sharp, suspicious eyes, and that they dwelt upon him altogether too attentively for a perfectly justifiable interest even in the box of grub.

Black coffee, drunk hot and strong, gave the world a brighter aspect. Casey decided that the situation was not so desperate, after all. Easy enough to bluff it out—easiest thing in the world! He would just go along as if there wasn't a thing on his mind heavier than his thinning, sandy hair. No man living had any right or business snooping around in his car, unless he carried a badge of an officer of the law. Even with the badge, Casey told himself sternly, a man would have to show a warrant before he could touch a finger to his outfit.

Over his third cup of coffee Casey eyed the stranger guardedly. He did not look like an officer. He was not big and burly, with arrogant eyes and the hint of leashed authority in his tone. Instead, he was of medium height, owned a pair of shrewd gray eyes and an easy drawl, and was dressed in the half military style so popular with mining men, surveyors and others who can afford to choose what garb they will adopt for outdoor living.

He had shown a perfect familiarity with cooking over a campfire, and had fried the bacon in a manner which even Casey could not criticize. Before the coffee was boiled he had told Casey that his name was Mack Nolan. Immediately afterward he had grinned and added the superfluous information that he was Irish and didn't care who knew it.

"Well, I'm Irish, meself," Casey returned approvingly and with more than his usual brogue. "You can ask anybody if Casey Ryan has ever showed shame fer the blood that's in' 'im. 'Tis the Irish that never backs up from a rough trail or a fight." He poured a fourth cup of coffee into a chipped enamel cup and took his courage in his two hands. Mack Nolan, he assured himself optimistically, couldn't possibly know what lay hidden under the camp outfit in the Ford. Until he did know, he was harmless as anybody, so long as Casey kept an eye on him.

CHAPTER THIRTEEN

During the companionable smoke that followed breakfast, Casey learned that Mack Nolan had spent some time in Nevada, ambling through the hills, examining the geologic formation of the country with a view to possible future prospecting in districts yet undeveloped.

"The mineral possibilities of Nevada haven't been more than scratched," Mack Nolan observed, lying back with one arm thrown up under his head as a makeshift pillow and the other hand negligently attending to the cigarette he was smoking. His gray army hat was tilted over his eyes, shielding them from the sun while they dwelt rather studiously upon the face of Casey Ryan.

"Every spring I like to get out and poke around through these hills where folks as a rule don't go. Never did much prospecting—as such. Don't take kindly enough to a pick and shovel for that. What I like best is general field work. If I run across something rich, time enough then to locate a claim or two and hire a couple of strong backs to do the digging.

"I've been out now for about three weeks; and night before last, just as I stopped to make camp and before I'd started to unpack, my two mules got scared at a rattler and quit the country. Left me flat, without a thing but my clothes and six-shooter, and what I had in my pockets." He lifted the cigarette from between his lips—thin, they were, and curved and rather pitiless, one could guess, if the man were sufficiently roused.

"I wasted all yesterday trying to trail 'em. But you can't do much tracking in these rocks back here toward the river. I was hitting for the highway to catch a ride if I could, when I saw you topping this last ridge over here. Don't blame me much for bumming a breakfast, do you?" And he added, with a sigh of deep physical content, "It sure-lee was some feed!"

His lids drooped lower as if sleep were overtaking him in spite of himself. "I'd ask yuh if you'd seen anything of those mules—only I don't give a damn now. I wish this was night instead of noon; I could sleep the clock around after that bacon and bannock of yours. Haven't a care in the world," he murmured drowsily. "Happy as a toad in the sun, first warm day of spring. How soon you going to crank up?"

Casey stared at him unwinkingly through narrowed lids. He pushed his hat forward with a sharp tilt over his eyebrow—which meant always that Casey Ryan had just O. K.'d an idea—and reached for his chewing tobacco.

"Go ahead an' take a nap if yuh want to," he urged. "I got some tinkerin' to do on the Ford, an' I was aimin' to lay over here an' do it. I'm kinda lookin' around, myself, for a likely prospect; I got all the time there is. I guess I'll back the car down the draw a piece where she'll set level, an' clean up 'er dingbats whilst you take a sleep."

Casey left the breakfast things where they were, as a silent reassurance to Mack Nolan that the car would not go off without him. It was a fine, psychological detail of which Casey was secretly rather proud. A box of grub, a smoked coffee pot and dirty breakfast dishes left beside a dead campfire establishes evidence, admissible before any jury, that the owner means to return.

Casey went over and cranked the Ford, grimly determined to make the coffee pot lie for him if necessary. He backed the car down the draw a good seventy-five yards, to where a wrinkle in the bank hid him from the breakfast camp. He stopped there and left the engine running while he straddled out over the side and went forward to the dip of the front fender to see if the Ford were still visible to Mack Nolan. He was glad to find that by crouching and sighting across the fender he could just see the campfire and the top of Nolan's hat beyond it. The man need only lift his head off his arm to see that the Ford was standing just around the turn of the draw.

"The corner was never yet so tight that Casey Ryan couldn't find a crack somewhere to crawl through," he told himself vaingloriously. "An' I hope to thunder the feller sleeps long an' sleeps solid!"

For fifteen minutes the mind of Casey Ryan was at ease. He had found a shovel in the car, placed conveniently at the side where it could be used for just such an emergency as this. For fifteen minutes he had been using that shovel in a shelving bank of loose gravel just under an outcropping of rhyolite a rod or so behind the car and well out of sight of Nolan.

He was beginning to consider his excavation almost deep enough to bury two ten-gallon kegs and forty bottles of whisky, when the shadow of a head and shoulders fell across the hole. Casey did not lift the dirt and rocks he had on his shovel. He froze to a tense quiet, goggling at the shadow.

"What are yuh doing, Casey? Trying to outdig a badger?" Mack Nolan's chuckle was friendliness itself.

Casey's head snapped around so that he could cock an eye up at Nolan. He grinned mechanically. "Naw. Picked up a rich-lookin' piece uh float. Thought I'd just see if it didn't mebby come from this ledge."

Mack Nolan stepped forward interestedly and looked at the ledge.

"Where's the piece you found?" he very naturally inquired. "The formation just here wouldn't lead me to expect gold-bearing rock; but of course, anything is possible with gold. Let's have a look at the specimen."

Casey had once tried to bluff a stranger with two deuces and a pair of fives, and two full stacks of blue chips pushed to the center to back the bluff. The stranger had called him, with three queens and a pair of jacks. Casey felt like that now.

He had laughed over his loss then, and he grinned now and reached carelessly to the bank beside him as if he fully expected to lay his hand on the specimen of gold-bearing rock. He went so far as to utter a surprised oath when he failed to find it. He felt in his pockets. He went forward and scanned the top of the ledge almost convincingly. He turned and stood a-straddle, his hands on his hips, and gazed on the pile of dirt he had thrown out of the hole. Last, he pushed his hat back so that with the next movement he could push it forward again over his eyebrow.

"Now if that there lump uh high-grade ain't went an' slid down the bank an' got covered up with the muck!" he exclaimed disgustedly. "I'm a son of a gun if Fate ain't playin' agin' Casey Ryan with a flock uh aces under its vest!"

Mack Nolan laughed, and Casey slanted a look his way. "Thought I left you takin, a nap," he said brazenly. "What's the matter? Didn't your breakfast set good?"

Mack Nolan laughed again. It was evident that he found Casey Ryan very amusing.

"The breakfast was fine," he replied easily. "A couple of lizards got to playing tag over me. That woke me up, and the sun was so hot I just thought I'd come down and crawl into the car and go to sleep there. Go ahead with your prospecting, Casey—I won't bother you."

Casey went on with his digging, but his heart was not in it. With every laggard shovelful of dirt, he glanced over his shoulder apprehensively, watching Mack Nolan crawl into the back of the car and settle himself, with an audible sigh of satisfaction, on top of the load. He had one wild, wicked impulse to lengthen the hole and make it serve as a grave for more than bootleg whisky; but it was an impulse born of desperation, and it died almost before it had lived.

CHAPTER FOURTEEN

Casey left his digging and returned to the Ford, still determined to carry on the bluff and pretend that much tinkering was necessary before he could travel further. With a great show of industry he rummaged for pliers and wrenches, removed the hood from the motor and squinted down at the little engine.

By that time Mack Nolan was snoring softly in deep slumber. Casey listened suspiciously, knowing too well how misleading a snore could be. But his own eyelids were growing exceeding heavy, and the soporific sound acted hypnotically upon his sleep-hungry brain. He caught himself yawning, and suddenly threw down the wrench.

"Aw, hell!" he muttered disgustedly, and went and crawled under the back of the car where it was shady.

The sun was nearly down when Casey awoke and crawled out. Mack Nolan was still curled comfortably in the car, his back against the bed roll. He opened his eyes and yawned when Casey leaned and looked in upon him.

"By Jove, that was a fine sleep I had," he announced cheerfully, lifting himself up and dangling his legs outside the car. "Strike anything yet?"

"Naw." Casey's grunt was eloquent of the mood he was in.

"Get the car fixed all right?" Mack Nolan's cheerfulness seemed nothing less than diabolical to Casey.

"Naw." Then Casey added grimly, "I'm stuck. I dunno what ails the damned thing. Have to send to Vegas fer new parts, I guess. It's only three miles out here to the road. Mebby you better hike over to the highway an' ketch a ride with somebody. I might send in for a timer an' some things, too. No use waitin' fer me, Nolan—can't tell how long I'll be held up here."

Mack Nolan climbed out of the car. Casey's spirits rose instantly. Nolan came forward and looked down at the engine as casually as he would glance at a nickel alarm clock.

"She was hitting all right when you backed down here," Nolan remarked easily. "I'll just take a look at her myself. Fords are cranky sometimes. But I've assembled too many of them in the factory to let one get the best of me in the desert."

Casey could almost hear his heart when it slumped down into his boots. But he wasn't licked yet.

"Aw, let the darned thing alone till we eat," he said, pushing his hat forward to hurry his wits.

"Well—I can throw a Ford together in the dark, if necessary," smiled Mack Nolan. "Eat, it is, if you want it that way. That breakfast I put away seems to have sharpened my appetite for supper. Tell you what, Ryan. I'll do a little trouble-shooting here while you cook supper. How'll that be?"

That wouldn't be, if Casey could prevent it. His pale, narrow-lidded eyes dwelt upon Nolan unwinkingly.

"Well, mebby I'm kind of a crank about my car," he hedged, with a praiseworthy calmness. "Fords is like horses, to me. I drove stage all m' life till I took to prospectin'—an' I never could stand around and let anybody else monkey with my teams. I ain't a doubt in the world, Mr. Nolan, but what you know as much about Fords as I do. More, mebby. But Casey Ryan's got 'is little ways, an' he can't seem to ditch 'em. We'll eat; an' then mebby we'll look 'er over together.

"At the same time," he went on with rising courage, "I'm liable to stick around here for awhile an' prospect a little. If you wanta find them mules an' outfit, don't bank too strong on Casey Ryan. He's liable to change 'is mind any old time. Day or night, you can't tell what Casey might take a notion to do. That there's a fact. You can ask anybody if it ain't."

Mack Nolan laughed and slapped Casey unexpectedly on the shoulder. "You're a man after my own heart, Casey Ryan," he declared enigmatically. "I'll stick to you and take a chance. Darn the mules! Somebody will find them and look after them until I show up."

Casey's spirits, as he admitted to himself, were rising and falling like the hammer of a pile driver; and like the pile driver, the hammer was driving him deeper and deeper into hopelessness. He would have given an ear to know for certain whether Mack Nolan were as innocent and friendly as he seemed. Until he did know, Casey could see nothing before him but to wait his chance to give Nolan the slip.

Sitting cross-legged in the glow of the campfire after supper, with a huge pattern of stars drawn over the purple night sky, Casey pulled out the old pipe with which he had solaced many an evening and stuffed it thoughtfully with tobacco. Across the campfire, Mack Nolan sat with his hat tilted down over his eyes, smoking a cigarette and seeming at peace with all the world.

Casey hoped that Nolan would forget about fixing the Ford. He hoped that Nolan would sleep well to-night. Casey was perfectly willing to sacrifice a good roll of bedding and the cooking outfit for the privilege of traveling alone. No man, he told himself savagely, could ask a better deal than he was prepared to give Nolan. He bent to reach a burning twig for his pipe, and found Nolan watching him steadily from under his hat brim.

"What sort of looking fellows were those, Ryan, that left a load of booze on your hands?" Nolan asked casually when he saw that he was observed.

Casey burned his fingers with the blazing twig. "Who said anything about any fellers leavin' me booze?" he evaded sharply. "If it's a drink you're hintin' for, you won't get it. Casey Ryan ain't no booze peddler, an' now's as good a time as any to let that soak into your system."

Mack Nolan's gray eyes were still watching Casey with a steadfastness that was disconcerting to a man in Casey's dilemma.

"It might help us both considerably," he said quietly, "if you told me all about it. You can't cache that booze you've got in the car—I won't let you, for one thing; for another, that would be merely dodging the issue, and if you'll forgive my frankness, dodging doesn't seem to be quite in your line."

Casey puffed hard on his pipe. "The world's gittin' so darned full uh crooks, a man can't turn around now'days without bumpin' into a few!" he exploded bitterly. "What kind uh hold-up game YOU playin', Mr. Nolan? If that's your name," he added fiercely.

Mack Nolan laughed to himself and rubbed the ash from his cigarette against the sole of his shoe. "Why," he answered genially, "my game is holding up bootleggers—and crooked cops. Speaking off-hand (which I don't often do) I should say you have a fine chance to sit in with me. I'm just guessing, now," he added dryly, "but I'm tolerably good at guessing; a man's got to be, these days."

"A man's got to do better than guess—with Casey Ryan," Casey remarked ominously. "The last man that guessed Casey Ryan, guessed 'im plumb wrong."

"Meaning that you'd refuse to help me round up bootleggers and the officers that protect them?" A steel edge crept into Mack Nolan's voice. He leaned forward, his elbows on his knees, his eyes boring into Casey's mind.

"Man, don't stall with me! You've got brains enough to know that if I were a crook I'd have held you up long before now. You gave me three splendid opportunities to stick a gun in your back—and I could have made others. And," he added with a smile, "if I had thought that you were a bootlegger or a crook of any other kind, I'd have had you in Las Vegas jail by this time. You're no more a crook than I am. You've got neither the looks nor the actions of a slicker. I may say I know you pretty well—"

Casey thrust out a pugnacious chin. "Say! D' you know Bill Masters, too? That's all I wanta know!"

"Bill Masters? Why, is he the fellow who stepped out from under this load of hootch? If he is, he must have picked himself a new name; I never heard it."

Casey glared suspiciously for twenty seconds before he settled back glumly into his mental corner.

"Ryan, I've been all day sizing you up. I'm going to be perfectly honest with you and tell you why I think you're straight—although you must admit the evidence is rather against you.

"I happened to be right close when you drove down in here and stopped. As a matter of fact, I was behind that little clump of junipers. Had you driven around them instead of stopping this side, you couldn't have failed to see me.

"You came down here mad at the trick that had been played you. You were so mad, you started talking to yourself as a safety valve—blowing off mental steam. You've spent a lot of time in the desert—alone. Men like that frequently talk aloud their thoughts, just to hear a human voice. You made matters pretty plain to me before you knew there was any one within miles of you. For instance, you're not at all sure this car you've got wasn't stolen. You're inclined to think it was. You're broke—robbed, I take it, by the men who somehow managed to leave you with the car and a load of booze on your hands. The trick must have been turned this morning; down at the railroad, I imagine—because you hadn't taken time to stop and size up the predicament you were in until you got here.

"Your main idea was to get off somewhere out of sight. You were scared. You didn't hear me behind you until I spoke—which proves you're a green hand at dodging. And that, Ryan, is a very good recommendation to a man in my line of work. But you're shrewd, and you're game—dead game. You're a peach at thinking up schemes to get yourself out of a hole. Of course, being new at it, you don't think quite far enough. For instance, because you found me afoot it never occurred to you that I might know something about a car; but the rest of your plan was a dandy.

"Your idea of backing down there around the turn and burying the booze was all right. With almost any other man it would have worked. Once you got that hootch off your mind, I rather think you'd have been glad to have me along with you, instead of giving me broad hints to leave. But you haven't got the booze buried yet, and you've been figuring all the evening. You don't see how the devil you're going to manage it with me around.

"I'll do a little more guessing, now: I guess you've doped it out that you'll pack the bedroll up here, tuck me in and pray to the Lord I'll sleep sound. You're hoping you can cache the booze and make your getaway while I've gone bye-low. Or possibly, if you got the booze put away safe from my prying eyes, you might come back to bed and I'd find you here in the morning just as if nothing had happened. How Is that for guesswork?"

"You go tahell!" growled Casey, swallowing a sickly grin. He pressed down the tobacco in his pipe, eyeing Nolan queerly. "If them damn' lizards had uh let yuh alone, I wouldn't have nothin' on m' mind now but my hat." He looked across the fire and grinned again.

"Keep on; you'll be tellin' me what the missus an' I was arguin' about last night over long-distance. I've heard tell uh this four-bit mind reading an' forecastin' your horrorscope fer a dime; but I never met up with it before. If you're aimin' to take up a collection after the show, you'll fare slim. I've been what a feller called 'dusted off'." He added, after a pause that was eloquent, "They done it thorough!"

Mack Nolan laughed. "They usually are thorough, when they're 'dusting off a chump', as I believe they call it."

Casey grunted. "'Chump' is right, mebby. But anyways, you're too late, Mr. Nolan. I'm cleaned."

Mack Nolan rolled another cigarette, lighted it and flipped the match into the campfire. He smoked it down to the last inch, staring into the fire and saying nothing the while. When the cigarette stub followed the match, he leaned back upon one elbow and began tracing a geometrical figure in the sand with a stick.

"Ryan," he said abruptly, "you're square and I know it. The very nature of my business makes me cautious about trusting men—but I'm going to trust you." He stopped again, taking great pains with the point of a triangle he was drawing.

Casey knocked the ashes out of his pipe against a rock. "Puttin' it that way, Mr. Nolan, the man's yet to live that Casey Ryan ever double-crossed. Cops I got no use for; nor yet bootleggers. Whether I got any use for you, Mr. Nolan, I can say better when I've heard yuh out. A goat I've been for the last time. But I'm willin' to HEAR yuh out—and that there's more'n what I'd uh said this morning."

"And that's fair enough, Ryan. If you jumped into things with your eyes shut, I don't think I'd want you with me."

Casey squirmed, remembering certain times when he had gone too headlong into things.

"I'm going to ask you, Ryan, to tell me the whole story of this car and its load of whisky. Before you do that, I'll tell you this much to show good faith and prove to you how much I trust you: I'm an officer, and my special work right now is to clean up a gang of bootleggers and the crooked officers who are protecting them. What I know about your case leads me to believe that you've run afoul of them and that you're the man I've been looking for that can help me set a trap for them. Would you like to do that?"

"If it's that bunch you're after, Mr. Nolan, I'd ruther land 'em in jail than to find a ledge of solid gold ten feet thick an' a mile long. One thing I'd like to know first. Are yuh or ain't yuh huntin' mules?"

Mack Nolan laughed. "I am, yes. But the mule I'm hunting is white!"

Casey studied that until he had the fresh pipeful of tobacco going well. Then he looked up and grinned understandingly.

"So it's White Mule you're trailin'." He kicked a stub of greasewood branch back into the flames and laughed. "Well, the tracks is deep an' plenty, and if that's the trail you're takin', I'm with yuh. You ain't a cop—leastways you don't spread your arms every time you turn around. Gosh, I hate them wing-floppin' kind! They's one thing an' one only that I hate worse—an' that's bootleggers an' moonshiners. If you got a scheme to give them cusses their needin's, you can ask anybody if Casey Ryan ain't the feller you can bank on."

"Yes. That's what I've been thinking. Now, I wish you'd tell me exactly what you've been up against. Don't leave out anything, however trivial it might seem to you."

Wherefore, Casey sat with the firelight flickering across his seamed, Irish face and told the story of his wrongs. Trivial details Nolan had asked for—and he got them with the full Casey Ryan flavor. Even the old woman who rocked, Casey pictured—from his particular angle. Mack Nolan sat up and listened, his eyes steady and his mouth, that had curved to laughter many times during the recital, once more firm and somewhat pitiless when Casey finished.

"This Smiling Lou; you'd know him again, of course?"

"Know him! Say, I'd know him after he'd fried a week in hell!" Casey's tone left no doubt of his meaning.

"And I suppose you could tell this man Kenner a mile off and around a corner. Now, I'll tell you what I want you to do, Casey. This may jar you a little—until I explain. I want you—" Mack Nolan paused, his lips twitching in a faint smile—"to do a little bootlegging yourself."

"Yuh—WHAT?" In the firelight Casey's eyes were seen to bulge.

"I want you to bootleg this whisky you've got in the car." Nolan's eyes twinkled. "I want you to go back and peddle this booze, and I want you to do it so that Smiling Lou or one of his bunch will hold you up and highjack you. Do you see what I mean? You don't—so I'll tell you. We'll put it in marked bottles. I have the bottles and the seals and labels for every brand of liquor to be had in the country to-day. With marked money and marked bottles, we ought to be able to get the goods on that gang."

Casey thought of something quite suddenly and held out an imperative, pointing finger.

"There's something else that feller told me was in the car!" he cried agitatedly. "He said he had forty pints of French champagne cached in a false bottom under the front seat. And he said the front cushion had a blind pocket around the edges that was full uh dope. Hop, he called it."

Mack Nolan whistled under his breath.

"And he turned the whole outfit over to you for sixteen hundred dollars or so?" He stared thoughtfully into the fire. Abruptly he looked at Casey.

"What the deuce had you done to him, Ryan?" he asked, with a quizzical intentness. "He must have been scared stiff, to let go of all that stuff for sixteen hundred. Why, man, the 'junk'—that's dope—alone must be worth more than that. And the champagne—forty pints, you say? He ought to get twenty dollars a pint for that. Figure it yourself. I hope," he added seriously, "the fellow wasn't too scared to show up again."

"Well," Casey said grimly, "I dunno how scart he is—but he knows darn' well I'll kill 'im. I told im I would."

Again Mack Nolan laughed. "Catching's much better than killing, Ryan. It hurts a man worse, and it lasts a heap longer. What do you say to turning in? To-morrow we'll have a full day at my private bottling works."

They moved their cooking outfit down near the Ford for safety's sake. While it was wholly improbable that the car would be robbed in the night, Mack Nolan was a man who took as few chances as possible. It happened that the excavation Casey had so hopefully made that morning formed a convenient level for their bed; wherefore they spread it there, talking in low tones of their plans until they went to sleep.

CHAPTER FIFTEEN

Dawn was just thinning the curtain of darkness when Nolan woke Casey with a shake of the shoulder.

"I think we'd better be moving from here before the world's astir. You can back on down this draw, Ryan, and strike an old trail that cuts over the ridge and up the next gulch to an old, deserted mine where I've made headquarters. It isn't far, and we can have breakfast at my camp."

Casey swallowed his astonishment, and for once in his life he did as he was told without argument.

Mack Nolan's camp was fairly accessible by roundabout trail with a few tire tracks to point the way for Casey. Straight across the ridges, it would not have been more than two miles to Juniper Wells. Nevertheless not one man in a year would be tempted to come this way, unless it were definitely known that some one lived here.

As the camp of a man who was prospecting for pastime rather than for a grubstake, the place was perfect. Mack Nolan had taken possession of a cabin dug into the hill at the head of a long draw. A brush-covered shed of makeshift construction sheltered a car of the ubiquitous Ford make. Fifty yards away and in full sight of the cabin, the mouth of a tunnel yawned blackly under a rhyolite ledge.

Casey swept the camp with an observant glance and nodded approval as and stopped before the cabin.

"As a prospector, Mr. Nolan, I'll say 'tis a fine layout you got here. An' tain't the first time an honest-lookin' mine has been made to cover things far off from minin'. Like the Black Butte bunch, f'r instance. But if any one was to ride up on yuh unexpected here, I'll say yuh could meet 'em with a grin an' feel easy about your secrets."

"That's praise indeed, coming from an old hand like you," Nolan declared. "Now I'll tell you something else. With Casey Ryan in the camp the whole thing's twice as convincing. Come in. I want to show you what I call an artistic interior."

Grinning, Casey followed him inside and exclaimed profanely in admiration of Mack Nolan's genius. The cabin showed every mark of the owner's interest in the geologic formation of that immediate district.

On the floor along the wall lay specimens of mineralized rock, a couple of prospector's picks, a single-jack and a set of drills; a sample sack, grimed and with a hole in the corner mended by the simple process of gathering the cloth together around it and tying it tightly with a string, hung from a nail above the tools. On the window sill were specimens of ore; two or three of the pieces showed a richness that lighted Casey's eyes with the enthusiasm of an old prospector. Mining journals and a prospector's manual lay upon a box table at the foot of the bunk. For the rest, the cabin looked exactly what it was—the orderly home of a man quite accustomed to primitive living far off from his fellows.

They had a very satisfactory breakfast cooked by Mack Nolan from his own supplies and eaten in a leisurely manner while Nolan talked of primary formations and secondary, and of mineral intrusions and breaks. Casey listened and learned a few things he had not known, for all his years of prospecting. Mack Nolan, he decided, could pass anywhere as a mining expert.

"And now," said Nolan briskly, when he had hung up the dishpan and draped the dishcloth over it to dry, "I'll show you the bottling works. We'll have to do the work by lantern-light. There's not one chance in fifty that any one would show up here—but you never can tell. We could get the stuff out of sight easily enough while the car was coming up the gulch. But the smell is a different matter. We'll take no chances."

At the head of the bunk, a curtained space beneath a high shelf very obviously did duty as a wardrobe. A leather motor coat hung there, one sleeve protruding beyond the curtain of flowered calico. Other garments bulged the cloth here and there. Nolan, smiling over his shoulder at Casey, nodded and pushed the clothing aside. A door behind opened inward, admitting the two into a small recess from which another door opened into a cellar dug deep into the hill.

Undoubtedly this had once been used as a frost-proof storeroom. A small ventilator pipe opened—so Nolan told Casey—in the middle of a greasewood clump. Nolan lighted a gasoline lantern that shed a white brilliance upon the room. On the long table which extended down one side of the room, Casey saw boxes of bottles and other supplies which he did not at the moment recognize.

"We'll have to rebottle all the whisky," said Nolan.

"You'll see a certain mark blown into the bottom of each one of these. The champagne, I'm afraid, I must either confiscate and destroy or run the risk of marking the labels. The hop we'll lay aside for further consideration."

Casey grinned, thinking of the speedy downfall of his enemies, Smiling Lou and Kenner—and, as a secondary consideration other crooks of their type.

"So now we'll unload the stuff, Ryan, and get to work here." Nolan adjusted the white flame in the mantle of the gasoline lantern and led the way outside. "Take in the seat-cushion, Casey. I don't fancy opening it outside, even in this howling wilderness."

"I think I'll just pack in the kegs first, Mr. Nolan." For the first time since the shock of Mr. Nolan's "mind-reading" the night before, Casey ventured a suggestion. "Anybody comes along, it's the kegs they'd look at cross-eyed. Cushions is expected in Fords—if I ain't buttin' in," he added meekly.

"Which you're not. You're acting as my agent now, Ryan, and it will take two heads to put this over without a hitch. Sure, put the kegs out of sight first. The bottles next—and then we'll make short work of the dope in the cushion."

Casey carried in the kegs while Nolan kept watch for inopportune visitors. It was thought inadvisable to unload the camp outfit from the car until the whisky was all removed. The outfit effectually hid what was below—and they were taking no chances. They both breathed freer when the two kegs were in the cellar. Nolan was pleased; too, when Casey came out with the sample bag and announced that he would carry the bottles in the bag. Then Nolan fancied he heard a car, and walked away to where he would have a longer view down the gulch. He would whistle, he said, and warn Casey if someone was coming.

He had not proceeded fifty yards when Casey yelled and brought him back at a run. Casey was rummaging in the car, throwing things about with a recklessness which ill-became an agent of the self-possessed Mack Nolan.

"There ain't a damn' bottle here!" he bellowed indignantly. "Them crooks gypped me outa ten gallons uh good, bottle whisky! Now what do you know about that, Mr. Nolan? That feller said it was high-grade stuff he had packed away at the bottom. He lied. There ain't nothin' here but a set uh skid chains an' a jack. An' the champagne, mebby, under the front seat!"

Mack Nolan's eyes narrowed. "I think Ryan, I'll have a look under that front seat."

He had a look—several looks, in fact. There was the false bottom under the seat, but there was nothing in it. He took his pocket knife, opened a blade and split the edge of the seat-cushion at the bottom. He inserted a finger and thumb and drew out a bit of hair stuffing. He stood up and eyed Casey sharply, and Casey stared back defensively.

"He was a darned liar from start t' finish. He said there was champagne an' he said there was hop," Casey stated flatly.

"I wondered at his letting go of stuff as valuable as that," said Nolan. "I think we'd better take a look at those kegs."

They went into the cellar and took a look at the kegs. Both kegs. Afterward they stood and looked at each other. Casey's hands went to his hips, and the muscles along his jaw hardened into lumps. He spat into the dirt of the cellar floor.

"Water!" He snorted disgustedly. "Casey Ryan with the devil an' all scart outa him, thinkin' he had ownership of a load uh booze an' hop sufficient t' hang 'im!" His hand slid into his trousers pocket, reaching for the comforting plug of tobacco. "Stuck up an' robbed is what happens t' Casey. You can ask anybody if it ain't highway robbery!"

Nolan stopped whistling under his breath. "There's the Ford," he reminded Casey comfortingly.

"Which I wisht it wasn't!" snarled Casey. "You know yourself, Mr. Nolan, it's likely stole, an' the first man I meet in the trail'll likely take it off me, claimin' it's his'n!"

Mack Nolan started whistling again, but checked himself abruptly. "Well, our trap's wanting bait, I see. This leaves me still hunting the White Mule."

"Aw, tahell with your White Mule! Tahell with everything!" Casey kicked the nearest keg viciously and went out into the sunshine, swearing to himself.

CHAPTER SIXTEEN

In the shade of a juniper that grew on the highest point of the gulch's rim, Mack Nolan lay sprawled on the flat of his back, one arm for a pillow, and stared up into the serene blue of the sky with cottony flakes of cloud swimming steadily to the northeast. Three feet away, Casey Ryan rested on left hip and elbow and stared glumly down upon the cabin directly beneath them. Whenever his pale, straight-lidded eyes focussed upon the dusty top of the Ford car standing in front of the cabin, Casey said something under his breath. Miles away to the south, pale violet, dreamlike in the distance, the jagged outline of a small mountain range stood as if painted upon the horizon. A wavy ribbon of smudgy brown was drawn uncertainly across the base of the mountains. This, Casey knew, when his eyes lifted to look that way, marked the line of the Sante Fe and a train moving heavily upgrade to the west.

Toward it dipped the smooth stretch of barren mesa cut straight down the middle with a yellow line that was the highway up which Casey had driven the morning before. The inimitable magic of distance and high desert air veiled greasewood, sage and sand with the glamour of unreality. The mountains beyond, unspeakably desolate and forbidding at close range, and the little black buttes standing afar, off—small spewings of age-old volcanos dead before man was born—seemed fascinating, unknown islets anchored in a sea of enchantment. Across the valley to the west nearer mountains, all amethyst and opal tinted, stood bold and inscrutable, with jagged peaks thrust into the blue to pierce and hold the little clouds that came floating by. Even the gulch at hand had been touched by the enchanter's wand and smiled mysteriously in the vivid sunlight, the very air a-quiver with that indescribable beauty of the high mesa land which holds desert dwellers in thrall.

When first Casey saw the smoke smudge against the mountains to the south, he remembered his misadventure of the lower desert and swore. When he looked again, the majestic sweep of distance gave him a satisfied feeling of freedom from the crowded pettinesses of the city. For the first time since trouble met him in the trail between Victorville and Barstow, Casey heaved a sigh of content because he was once more out in the big land he loved. Those distant, painted mountains, looking as impossible as the back drop of a stage, held gulches and deep canyons he knew. The closer hills he had prospected. The mesa, spread all around him, seemed more familiar than the white apartment house in Los Angeles which Casey had lately called home. And if the thought of the Little Woman brought with it the vague discomfort of a schoolboy playing hookey, Casey could not have regretted being here with Mack Nolan if he had tried.

They were lying up here in the shade—following the instinct of other creatures of the wild to guard against surprises—while they worked out a nice problem in moonshine. And since the desert had never meant a monotonously placid life to Casey—who carried his problems philosophically as a dog bears patiently with fleas—he had every reason now for feeling very much at home. When he reached mechanically into his pocket for his Bull Durham and papers, any man who knew him well would have recognized the motion as a sign that Casey was himself again, once more on his mental feet and ready to go boring optimistically into his next bunch of trouble.

Mack Nolan raised his head off his arm and glanced at Casey quizzically.

"Well—we can't catch fish if we won't cut bait," he volunteered sententiously. "I've a nice little job staked out for you, Casey."

Casey gave a grunt that might mean one of several things, and which probably meant them all. He waited until he had his cigarette going. "If it ain't a goat's job I'm fer it," he said. "Casey Ryan ain't the man t' set in the shade whilst there's men runnin' loose he's darned anxious t' meet."

"I've been thinking over the deal those fellows pulled on you. If the man Kenner had left you the booze and dope he told you was in the car, I'd say it was a straight case of a sticky-fingered officer letting a bootlegger by with part of his load, and a later attack of cold feet on the part of the bootlegger. But they didn't leave you any booze. So I have doped it this way, Ryan.

"The thing's deeper than it looked, yesterday. Those two were working together, part of a gang, I should say, with a fairly well-organized system. By accident—and probably for a greater degree of safety in getting out of the city, Kenner invited you to ride with him. He wanted no argument with that traffic cop—no record made of his name and license number. So he took you in. When he found out who you were, he knew you were at outs with the law. He knew you as an experienced desert man. He had you placed as a valuable member of their gang, if you could be won over and persuaded to join them.

"As soon as possible he got you behind the wheel—further protection to himself if he should meet an officer who was straight. He felt you out on the subject of a partnership. And when you met Smiling Lou—well, this Kenner had decided to take no chance with you. He still had hopes of pulling you in with them, but he was far from feeling sure of you. He undoubtedly gave Smiling Lou the cue to make the thing appear an ordinary case of highjacking while he ditched his whole load so that there would be no evidence against him if he lost out and you turned nasty.

"I'm absolutely certain, Casey, that if you had not been along, Smiling Lou would not have touched that load. They'd probably have stopped there for a talk, exchanged news and perhaps perfected future plans, and parted like two old cronies. It's possible, of course, that Smiling Lou might have taken some whisky back with him—if he had needed it. Otherwise, I think they split more cash than booze, as a rule."

Casey sat up. "Well, they coulda played me for a sucker easy enough," he admitted reluctantly. "An' if it'll be any help to yuh, Mr. Nolan, I'll say that I never seen the money passed from Kenner to Smilin' Lou, an' I never seen a bottle unloaded from the car. I heard 'em yes. An' I'll say there was a bunch of 'em all right. But what I SEEN was the road ahead of me and that car of Smilin' Lou's standin' in the middle of it. He had a gun pulled on me, mind yuh —and you can ask anybody if a feller feels like rubberin' much when there's only the click of a trigger between him an' a six-foot hole in the ground."

"All the more reason," said Nolan, also sitting up with his hands clasped around his knees, "why it's important to catch them with the goods. You'll have to peddle hootch, Casey, until we get Smiling Lou and his outfit."

"And where, Mr. Nolan, do I git the booze to peddle?" asked Casey practically.

Nolan laughed to himself. "It can be bought," he said, "but I'd rather not. Since you've never monkeyed with the stuff, it might make you conspicuous if you went around buying up a load of hootch. And of course I can't appear in this thing at all. But I have what I think is a very good plan."

Casey looked at him inquiringly, and again Nolan laughed.

"Nothing for it, Casey,—we'll have to locate a still and rob it. That, or make some of our own, which takes time. And it's an unpleasant, messy job anyway."

Casey stared dubiously down into the gulch. "That'd be fine, Mr. Nolan, if we knew where was the still. Or mebby yuh do know."

Mack Nolan shook his head. "No, I don't, worse luck. I haven't been long enough in the district to know as much about it as I hope to know later on. Prospecting for this headquarters took a little time; and getting my stuff moved in here secretly took more time. A week ago, Casey, I shouldn't have been quite ready to use you. But you came when you were needed, and so—I feel sure the White Mule will presently show up."

Casey lifted his head and stared meditatively out across the immensity of the empty land around them.

"She's a damn' big country, Mr. Nolan. I dunno," he remarked doubtfully. "But Casey Ryan has yet t' go after a thing an' fail t' git it. I guess if it's hootch we want, it ought t' be easy enough t' find; it shore has been hard t' dodge it lately! If yuh want White Mule, Mr. Nolan, you send Casey out travelin' peaceful an' meanin' harm t' nobody. Foller Casey and you'll find 'im tangled up with a mess uh hootch b'fore he gits ten miles from camp."

"You could go out and highjack some one." Nolan agreed, taking him seriously—which Casey had not intended. "I think we'll go down and load the camp outfit into my car, Ryan, and I'll start you out. Go up into your old stamping ground where people know you. If you're careful in picking your men, you could locate some hootch, couldn't you, without attracting attention?"

Casey studied the matter. "Bill Masters could mebby help me out," he said finally. "Only I don't like the friends Bill's been wishin' onto me lately. This man Kenner, that held me up, knowed Bill Masters intimate. I'm kinda losin' my taste fer Bill lately."

Mack Nolan seized upon the clue avidly. Before Casey quite realized what he had done, he found himself hustled away from camp in Mack Nolan's car, headed for Lund in the service of his government. Since young Kenner had been able to talk so intimately of Bill Masters, Mack Nolan argued that Bill Masters should likewise be able to give some useful information concerning young Kenner. Moreover, a man in Bill Masters' position would probably know at least a few of the hidden trails of the White Mule near Lund.

"If you can bring back a load of moonshine Ryan, by all means do so," Nolan instructed Casey at the last moment. "Here's money to buy it with. We should have enough to make a good haul for Smiling Lou. Twenty gallons at least— forty, if you can get them. Keep your weather eye open, and whatever happens, don't mention my name or say that you are working with the law. In five days, if you are not here, I shall drive to Las Vegas. Get word to me there if anything goes wrong. Just write or wire to General Delivery. But I look for you back, Ryan, not later than Friday midnight. Take no unnecessary risk; this is more important than you know."

Nolan's crisp tone of authority remained with Casey mile upon mile. And such was the Casey Ryan driving that midnight found him coasting into Bill Masters' garage in Lund with the motor shut off and a grin on the Casey Ryan face.

CHAPTER SEVENTEEN

Mack Nolan had just crawled into his bunk on Wednesday night when he thought he heard a car laboring up the gulch. He sat up in bed to listen and then got hurriedly into his clothes. He was standing just around the corner of the dugout where the headlights could not reach him, when Casey killed the engine and stopped before the door. Steam was rising in a small cloud from the radiator cap, and the sound of boiling water was distinctly audible some distance away.

Mack Nolan waited until Casey had climbed out from behind the wheel and headed for the door. Then he stepped out and hailed him. Casey started perceptibly, whirling as if to face an enemy. When he saw that it was Nolan he apparently lost his desire to enter the cabin. Instead he came close to Nolan and spoke in a hoarse whisper.

"We better run 'er under the shed, Mr. Nolan, and drain the darned radiator. I dunno am I follered or not, but I was awhile back. But the man that catches Casey Ryan when he's on the trail an' travelin, has yet t' be born. An' you can ask anybody if that ain't so."

Mack Nolan's eyes narrowed. "And who followed you then?" he asked quietly. "Did you bring any hootch?"

"Did yuh send Casey Ryan after hootch, or was it mebby spuds er somethin'?" Casey retorted with heavy dignity. "Will yuh pack it in, Mr. Nolan, whilst I back the car in the shed, or shall I bring it when I come? It ain't so much," he added drily, "but it cost the trouble of a trainload."

"I'll take it in," said Nolan. "If any one does come we want no evidence in reach."

Casey turned to the car, clawed at his camp outfit and lifted out a demijohn which he grimly handed to Nolan. "Fer many a mile it rode on the seat with me so I could drink 'er down if they got me cornered," he grinned. "One good swaller is about the size of it, Mr. Nolan."

Nolan grinned in sympathy and turned into the cabin, bearing the three-gallon, wicker-covered glass bottle in his arms. Presently he returned to the doorway and stood there listening down the gulch until Casey came up, walking from the shed.

"'Tis a good thing yuh left this other car standin' here cold an' peaceful, Mr. Nolan," Casey, observed, after he also had stood for a minute listening. "If they're follerin' they'll be here darn' soon. If they ain't I've ditched 'em. Let's git t' bed an' I'll tell yuh my tale uh woe."

Without a word Nolan led the way into the cabin. In the dark they undressed and got into the bed which was luckily wide enough for two.

"Had your supper?" Nolan asked belatedly when they were settled.

"I did not," Casey grunted. "I will say, Mr. Nolan, there's few times in my life when you'd see Casey Ryan missin' 'is supper whilst layin' tracks away from a fight. But if it was light enough you could gaze upon 'im now. And I must hand it t' the Gallopin' Gussie yuh give me the loan of fer the trip. She brung me home ahead of the sheriff—and you can ask anybody if Casey Ryan himself can't be proud uh that!"

"The sheriff?" Nolan's voice was puzzled. He seemed to be considering something for a minute, before he spoke again. "You could have explained to the sheriff, couldn't you, your reason for having booze in the car?"

Casey raised to one elbow. "When yuh told Casey Ryan 'twas not many men you'd trust, and that you trusted me an' the business was t' be secret—Mr. Nolan, you 'was talkin' t' CASEY RYAN!" He lay down again as if that precluded further argument.

"Good! I thought I hadn't made a mistake in my man," Nolan approved, in a tone that gave Casey an inner glow of pride in himself. "Let's have the story, old man. Did you see Bill Masters?"

"Bill Masters," said Casey grimly, "was not in Lund. His garage is sold an' Bill's in Denver—which is a long drive for a Ford t' git there an' back before Friday midnight. Yuh put a time limit me, Mr. Nolan, an' nobody had Bill's address. I didn't foller Bill t' Denver. I asked some others in Lund if they knowed a man named Kenner, and they did not. So then I went huntin' booze that I could git without the hull of Nevada knowin' it in fifteen minutes. An' Casey's got this t' say: When yuh WANT hootch, it's hard t' find as free gold in granite. When yuh DON'T want it, it's forced on yuh at the point of a gun. This jug I stole—seein' your business is private, Mr. Nolan.

"I grabbed it off some fellers I knowed in Lund an' never had no use for, anyway. They're mean enough when they're sober, an' when they're jagged they're not t' be mentioned on a Sunday. I mighta paid 'em for it, but money's no good t' them fellers an' there's no call t' waste it. So they made a holler and I sets the jug down an' licks them both, an' comes along home mindin' my own business.

"So I guess they 'phoned the sheriff in Vegas that here comes a bootlegger and land 'im quick. Anyway, I was goin' t' stop there an' take on a beefsteak an' a few cups uh coffee, but I never done it. I was slowin' down in front uh Sam's Place when a friend uh mine gives me the high sign t' put 'er in high an' keep 'er goin'. Which I done.

"Down by Ladd's, Casey looks back an' here comes the sheriff's car hell bent fer 'lection (anyway it looked like the sheriff's car). An' I wanta say right here, Mr. Nolan, that's a darn' good Ford yuh got! I was follered, and 'I was follered hard. But I'm here an' they' ain't—an' you can ask anybody if that didn't take some going'!"

In the darkness of the cabin Casey turned over and heaved a great sigh. On the heels of that came a chuckle.

"I got t' hand it t' the L. A. traffic cops, Mr. Nolan. They shore learned me a lot about dodgin'. So now yuh got the hull story. If it was the sheriff behind me an' if he trails me here, they got no evidence an' you can mebby square it with 'im. You'd know what t' tell 'im—which is more'n what Casey Ryan can say."

Casey fell asleep immediately afterward, but Mack Nolan lay for a long while with his eyes wide open and his ears alert for strange sounds in the gulch. He was a new man in this district, working independently of sheriff's offices. Casey Ryan was the first man he had confided in; all others were fair game for Nolan to prove honest or dishonest with the government. The very nature of his business made it so. For when whisky runners drove openly in broad daylight through the country with their unlawful loads, somewhere along the line officers of the law were sharing the profits. Nolan knew none of them,— by sight. If he carried the records of some safely memorized and pigeonholed for future use, that was his own business. Mack Nolan's thoughts were his own and he guarded them jealously and slept with his lips tightly closed. He wanted no sheriff coming to him for explanation of his movements. Wherefore he listened long, and when he slept his slumber was light.

At daylight he was up and abroad. Two hours after sunrise Casey awoke with the smell of breakfast in his nostrils. He rolled over and blinked at Mack Nolan standing with his hat on the back of his head and a cigarette between his lips, calmly turning three hot-cakes with a kitchen knife. Casey grinned condescendingly. He himself turned his cakes by the simple process of tossing them in the air a certain kind of flip, and catching them dexterously as they came down. Right there he decided that Mack Nolan was not after all a real outdoors man.

"Well, the sheriff didn't arrive last night," Nolan observed cheerfully, when he saw that Casey was awake. "I don't much look for him, either. Your driving on past the turn to Juniper Wells and coming up that other old road very likely threw him off the track. You must have been close to the State line then and he gave you up as a bad job."

"It was a GOOD job!" Casey maintained reaching for his clothes. "I made 'em think I was headed clean outa the country. If they knowed who it was at all, they'd know I belong in L. A., and I figured they'd guess I was headed there. They stopped for something this side of Searchlight an' so I pulls away from 'em a couple of miles. They never seen where I went to."

While he washed for breakfast, Casey began to take stock of certain minor injuries.

"That darned Pete Gibson has got tushes in his mouth like a wild hawg; the kind that sticks out," he grumbled, touching certain skinned places on his knuckles. "Every time I landed on 'im yesterday I run against them tushes uh his'n." But he added with a grin, "They ain't so solid as they was when I met up with 'im. I felt one of 'em give 'fore I got through."

"Brings the price of moonshine up a bit, doesn't it?" Nolan suggested drily. "I rather think you might better have paid the men their price. A fight is well enough in its way—I'm Irish myself. But as my agent, Ryan, the main idea is to let the law fight for you. Our work is merely to give the law a chance. I like your not wanting to explain to the sheriff. Prohibition officers do not explain, as a rule. The law behind them does that.

"And since the price seems to be rather hard on the knuckles—" He glanced down at Casey's hands and grinned. "—I think it may come cheaper to make the stuff ourselves. Licking two men for three gallons, and getting the officers at your tail light into the bargain, is all right as an experiment; but I don't believe, Ryan, we ought to adopt that as a habit."

Casey cocked an eye up at him. "Did yuh ever make White Mule, Mr. Nolan?" he asked grimly.

Nolan laughed his easy little chuckle. "Why, no, Ryan, I never did. Did you?"

"Naw. I seen some made once, but I had too much of it inside me at the time to learn the receipt for it. I'd rather steal it, if it's all the same to you, Mr. Nolan." His hand went up to the back of his head and moved forward, although there was no hat to push. "I've lived honest all these years—an', dammit, it's kinda tough to break out with stealin I what yuh don't want! Couldn't we fill them bottles with somethin' that LOOKS like hootch? Cold tea should get by, Mr. Nolan. It'd be a fine joke on Smilin' Lou."

"A good joke, maybe—but no evidence. It isn't against the law, Ryan, to have cold tea in your possession. No, it's got to be whisky, and there's got to be a load of it. Enough to look like business and tempt him or any other member of the gang you happen to meet. If they caught you with three gallons, Casey, they'd probably run you in and feel very virtuous about it. Nothing for it, I'm afraid. We'll have to become real moonshiners ourselves for awhile."

Casey ate with less appetite after that. Making moonshine did not appeal to him at all. Given his choice, I think he would even prefer drinking it, unhappy as the effect had been on him.

"We'll need a still, and we'll need the stuff. I'm going to leave you in charge of the camp, Ryan, while I make a trip to Needles. I'll deputize you to assist me in cleaning up this district. And this district, Ryan, touches salt water. So if revenge looks good to you, you'll have a fine chance to get even with the bootleggers. And in the meantime, just kill time around camp here while I'm gone. If any one shows up, you're prospecting."

That day, doubt-devils took hold of Casey Ryan and plucked at his belief. How did he know that Mack Nolan wasn't another bootlegger, wanting to rope Casey in on a job for some fell purpose of his own? He had Mack Nolan's word and nothing more. For that matter, he had also had young Kenner's word. Kenner had fooled him completely. Mack Nolan could also fool him—perhaps.

"Well, anyhow, he never claimed to know Bill Masters, and that's a point in 'is favor. And if it's some dirty work he's up to, he coulda made it shorter than what he's doin'. An' if he's double-crossin' Casey Ryan—well, anyway, Casey Ryan 'll be present at the time an' place when he does it!"

Upon that comforting thought, Casey decided to trust Mack Nolan until he caught him playing crooked; and proceeded to kill time as best he could.

CHAPTER EIGHTEEN

It was noon the next day when Nolan returned, and he did not explain why he was eighteen hours overdue. Casey eyed him expectantly, but Nolan's manner was brisk and preoccupied.

"Help me unload this stuff, Ryan," he said, "and put it out of sight in the cellar. We won't have to go through the process of making moonshine, after all."

Casey looked into the car, pulling aside the tarp. Four kegs he counted, and lifted out one.

"An' how many did YOU lick, Mr. Nolan?" he grinned over his shoulder as he started for the door.

Nolan laughed noncommittally.

"Perhaps I'm luckier at picking my bootleggers," he retorted. "If you carry the right brand of bluff, you can keep the skin on your knuckles, Ryan. This beats making it, at any rate."

That afternoon and the next day, Casey Ryan did what he never dreamed was possible. With Mack Nolan to show him how, Casey performed miracles. While he did not, literally change water into wine, he did give forty-three gallons of White Mule a most imposing pedigree.

He turned kegs of crude, moonshine whisky into Canadian Club, Garnkirk, Tom Pepper, Three Star Hennessey and Cognac—if you were to believe the bottles, labels and government seals. Under Mack Nolan's instruction and with his expert assistance, the forgery was perfect. While the cellar reeked with the odor of White Mule when they had finished, the bottled array on the table whispered of sybaritic revelings to glisten the eyes of the most dissipated man about town.

"When it's as easy done as that, Mr. Nolan, the feller's a fool that drinks it. You've learnt Casey Ryan somethin' that mighta done 'im some good a few years back." He picked up a flat, pint bottle and caressed its label with reminiscent finger tips.

"Many's the time me an' old Tommy Pepper drove stage together," he mused. "Throwed 'im at a bear once that I met in the trail over in Colorado when I hadn't no gun on me. Busted a pint on his nose—man! Then I never waited to see what happened. I was a wild divil them days when me an' Tommy Pepper was side pardners. But a yaller snake with a green head crawled out of a bottle of 'im once—and that there was where Casey Ryan says good-by to booze. If I hadn't quit 'im then, I'd sure as hell quit 'im now. After this performance, Mr. Nolan, Casey Ryan's goin' to look twice into his coffee pot. I wouldn't believe in cow's milk, if I done the milkin' myself!"

"Most of the stuff that's peddled nowadays is doctored," Nolan replied, with the air of one who knows. "When it isn't White Mule, it's likely to be something worse. That's one of the chief reasons why I'm fighting it. If they only peddled decent whisky it wouldn't be so bad, Ryan. But it's rank poison. I've seen so many go stone blind—or die—that it makes me pretty savage sometimes. So now I'll coach you in the part you're to play as hootch runner; and to-morrow you can start for Los Angeles."

Casey did not answer. He felt absently for his pipe, filled and lighted it and went out to sit on the doorstep in gloomy meditation while he smoked.

Returning to Los Angeles, even without a bootlegger's load, was not a matter which Casey liked to contemplate. He would have to face the Little Woman if he went back; either as a deliberate liar, who lied to his wife to gain the freedom he might have had without resorting to deceit, or as the victim once more of crooks. Casey thought he would prefer the accusation of lying deliberately to the Little Woman, though it made him squirm to think of it. He wished she had not openly taunted him with getting into trouble and needing her always to get him out.

He would like to tell her that he was now working for the government. The secrecy of his mission, the danger it involved, would impress even her amused cynicism. But the very secrecy of his mission in itself made it impossible for him to tell her anything about it. Casey would not admit it, but it was a real disappointment to him that he could not wear a star on his coat.

All that day and evening he was glum, a strange mood for Casey Ryan. But if Mack Nolan noticed his silence, he gave no sign. Nolan himself was wholly absorbed by the business in hand. The success of this plan meant a good deal to him, and he told Casey so very frankly; which lightened Casey's gloom perceptibly.

Casey was to drive to Los Angeles—even to San Diego if necessary—and return within a week, unless Nolan's hopes were fulfilled and Casey was held up and highjacked. If he were apprehended by officers who were honestly discharging their duty, Casey was to do thus-and-so, and presently be free to drive on with his load. If he were highjacked (Casey gritted his teeth and said he hoped the highjacker would be Smiling Lou), he was to permit himself to be robbed, worm himself as far as possible into their confidence and return for further orders.

If Mack Nolan should chance to be absent from the cabin, then Casey was to wait until he returned. And Nolan intimated that hereafter the making of moonshine might be a part of Casey's duties. Then, without warning, Mack Nolan struck at the heart of Casey's worry.

"I don't want to dictate to any man in family affairs, Ryan. But I've got to speak of one other matter," he said diffidently. "I suppose naturally you'll want to go home and let your wife know you're still alive, anyway. But if you can manage to keep your present business a secret for the time being, I think you'd better do it. You said you were planning to be away on a trip for some time, I remember. If you can just let it go that way, or say that you are prospecting over here, I wish you would. Think you can manage that all right?"

"I'd rather manage a six-horse team of bronk mules," Casey admitted. "But after the way the missus thinks I lied to 'er about takin' the next train home from Barstow, anything I say 'll be used agin' me. My wife's got brains. She ain't put it down that the trains have quit runnin'. Accordin' to her figures, Casey's lied and he's in a hole again, an' it'll be up to her an' Jack to run windlass an' pull 'im out. Don't matter what I say she won't believe me anyhow —so Casey won't say nothin'. Can't lie with your mouth shut, can yuh?"

"Oh, yes, it's been done," Mack Nolan chuckled. "Now we'll set down the serial numbers and the bank name of this 'jack',—and here's your expense money separate. And if there's anything that isn't clear to you, Ryan, speak up. You won't hear from me again, probably, until you're back from this fishing trip."

Casey thought that everything was perfectly clear, and rashly he said so, as he started off.

From Barstow to Victorville, from Victorville to Camp Cajon Casey drove expectantly, hoping to meet Smiling Lou. He scanned each car that approached and slowed for every meeting like a searching party or a man who is lost and wishes to inquire the way. His pace would have been law-abiding in Los Angeles at five o'clock on Broadway between Fourth and Eighth streets. Goggled women tourists eyed him curiously, and one car stopped full to see what he wanted. But his "Tom Pepper" rode safe under the tarp behind him, and the "Three Star Hennessey" beaded daintily with the joggling it got, and Casey was neither halted nor questioned as he passed.

At Camp Cajon Casey stopped and cooked an early supper, because the summer crowd was there and a real bootlegger would have considered stopping rather unsafe. Casey boiled coffee over one of the camp fireplaces and watched furtively the sunburned holiday group nearest. He placed his supper on one of the round, cement tables near the car, and every man who passed that way Casey watched unblinkingly while he ate.

He succeeded in making three different parties swallow their supper in a hurry and pack up and leave, glancing back uneasily at Casey as they drove away. But Casey himself was unmolested, and no one asked about his load.

From Camp Cajon to San Bernardino Casey drove furiously, remembering young Kenner's desire for speed. He stopped there for the night, and nearly had a fight with the garage man where he put up, because he showed undue caution concerning the safety of his car from prowlers during the night.

He left the car there that day and returned furtively after dark, asking the night man if he had seen any saps around his car. The night man looked at him uncomprehendingly.

"I dunno—nothin's been picked up since I come on at six. We ain't responsible for lost articles, anyway. See that sign?"

Casey grunted, cranked up and drove away, wondering whether the night man was as innocent as he tried to act.

From San Bernardino to Los Angeles Casey drove placidly as a load of oranges in February. He put up at a cheap place on San Pedro Street, with his car in the garage next door and a five-dollar tip in the palm of a rat-faced mechanic with Casey's injunction to clean 'er dingbats and keep other people away.

He did not go out to see the Little Woman, after all. He had sent her a wire from Goffs the day before, saying that he was prospecting with a fellow and he hoped she was well. This, after long pondering, had seemed to him the easiest way out of an argument with the Little Woman. The wire had given no address whereby she might reach him, but the omission was not the oversight Casey hoped she would consider it. He wanted to be reassuring without starting anything.

Los Angeles with no Little Woman at his elbow was a dismal hole, and Casey got out of it as soon as possible. As per instructions, he drove down to San Diego, ventured perilously close to the Mexico line, fooled around there for a day looking for trouble, failed to find so much as a frown and drove back.

He headed straight for San Bernardino, which was Smiling Lou's headquarters. He killed time there and met the sheriff on the street the day he arrived. The sheriff had a memory trained to hold faces indefinitely. He smiled a little, made a polite gesture in the general direction of his hat and passed on. Casey swore to himself and resolved to duck guiltily around the nearest corner if he saw the sheriff coming his way again.

On the day when his time limit expired Casey drove up the gulch to Nolan's camp. In the car behind him rode undisturbed his Canadian Club, Garnkirk, Three-Star Hennessey, Cognac and Tom Pepper; bottles, labels, government seals and all. Nolan was walking over from the tunnel when Casey arrived. He smiled inquiringly as he shook hands,—a ceremony to which Casey was plainly unaccustomed.

"What luck, Ryan? I beat you back by about two hours. Getting things ready to begin making it. Did they catch you all right?"

"Naw!" Casey spat disgustedly. "Never seen a booze peddler, never seen a cop look my way. I went around actin' like I just killed a man an' stole a lady's diamonds, and the sheriff at San Berdoo TIPS 'IS HAT TO ME, by golly! Drove through L. A. hella-whoopin' an' not a darned traffic cop knowed it was Casey Ryan. You can ask anybody if I didn't do every thing possible to git in bad or give bootleggers a tip I was one of 'em.

"You can't git Casey Ryan up agin' the gang you're after, Mr. Nolan. Only way Casey Ryan can git up agin' the law is to go along peaceable tryin' to please the missus an' mindin' his own business. I coulda peddled that damn' hootch on a hangin' tray like circus lemonade. I coulda stood on the corner in any uh them damned towns with the hull works piled out on a table in front of me, an' I coulda hollered my damn' head off; an' Smilin' Lou woulda passed me by like I was sellin' chewin' gum and shoe strings."

Mack Nolan looked at Casey, turned and went into the cabin, sat down on the edge of the bed and laughed until the tears dripped over his lashes. Casey Ryan followed him, and sat on the edge of the table with his arms folded. Whenever Mack Nolan lifted his face from his palms and looked at Casey, Casey swore. Whereat Mack Nolan would give another whoop.

You can't wonder if relations were somewhat strained, between them for the rest of that day.

CHAPTER NINETEEN

Nature had made Casey Ryan an optimist. The blood of Ireland had made him pugnacious. And Mack Nolan had a way with him. Wherefore, Casey Ryan once more came larruping down the grade to Camp Cajon and turned in there with a dogged purpose in his eyes and with his jaw set stubbornly. History has it that whenever Casey Ryan gets that look in his face, the man underneath might just as well holler and crawl out; because holler he must, before Casey would ever let him up.

Behind him, stowed under the bedding, grub and camp dishes, rode his eight cases of bootlegger's bait, packed convincingly in the sawdust, straw and cardboard of the wet old days when Uncle Sam himself O. K.'d the job. A chain of tiny beads at the top of each bottle lied and said it was good liquor. The boxes themselves said, "This side up"—when any side up would thrill the soul of the man who owned a wet appetite and a dry throat.

It was a good job Mack Nolan had made of the bottling. Uncle Sam himself must needs polish his spectacles and take another look to detect the fraud. It was a marvelous job of bottling,—and the proof lay only in the drinking. "Tommy" Pepper rode in pint flasks designed to slip safely into a man's coat pocket. Beside him two cases of Canadian Club (if you were satisfied with the evidence of your eyes) sat serene in round-shouldered bottles—conventional, secure in its reputation. Cognac and Garnkirk, a case for each, rode in tall, slim bottles with no shoulders at all. Plumper than they, Three Star Hennessey sat smugly waiting until the joke was turned upon its victim. A tempting load it was, to men of certain minds and morals. Casey grinned sardonically when he thought of it.

Casey drove deep into the grove of sycamores and made camp there, away from the chattering picnic parties at the cement tables. By Mack Nolan's advice he was adopting a slightly different policy. He no longer shunned his fellow men or glared suspiciously when strangers approached. Instead he was very nearly the old Casey Ryan, except that he failed to state his name and business to all and sundry with the old Casey Ryan candor, but instead avoided the subject altogether or evaded questions with vague generalities.

But as an understudy for Ananias, Casey Ryan would have been a failure. In two hours or less he had made easy trail acquaintance with six different men, and he had unconsciously managed to vary his vague account of himself six different times. Wherefore he was presently asked cautiously concerning his thirst.

"They's times," said Casey, hopefully lowering an eyelid, "when a feller dassent take a nip, no matter how thirsty he gits."

The questioner stared at him for a minute and slowly nodded. "You're darn' right," he assented. "I scursely ever touch anything, myself." And he added vaguely, "Quite a lot of it peddled out here in this camp, I guess. Tourists comin' through are scared to pack it themselves—but they sure don't overlook any chances to take a snort."

"Yeah?" Casey cocked a knowing eye at the speaker. "They must pay a pretty fair price fer it, too. Don't the cops bother folks none?"

"Some—I guess."

Casey filled his pipe and offered his tobacco sack to the man. The fellow took it, nodding listless thanks, and filled his own pipe. The two sat down together on the knee of a deformed sycamore and smoked in circumspect silence.

"Arizona, I see." The man nodded toward the license plates on Casey's car.

"Uh-huh." Casey glanced that way. "Know a man name of Kenner?" He asked abruptly.

The fellow looked at Casey sidelong, without turning his head.

"Some. Do you?"

"Some." Casey felt that he was making headway, though it was a good deal like playing checkers with the king row wide open and only two crowned heads to defend his men.

"Friend uh yours?" The fellow turned his head and looked straight at Casey.

Casey returned him a pale, straight-lidded stare. The man's glance flickered and swung away.

"Who wants to know?" Casey asked calmly.

"Oh, you can call me Jim Cassidy. I just asked." He removed his pipe from his mouth and inspected it apathetically. "He's a friend of Bill Masters, garage man up at Lund. Know Bill?"

"Any man says I don't, you can call 'im a liar." Casey also inspected his pipe. "Bought that car off'n Kenner," Casey added boldly. Getting into trouble, he discovered, carried almost the thrill of trying to keep out of it.

"Yeah?" The self-styled Jim Cassidy looked at the Ford more attentively. "And contents?"

Casey snorted. "What do you know about goats, if anything?" he asked mysteriously.

Jim Cassidy eyed Casey sidelong through a silence. Then he brought his palm down flat on his thigh and laughed.

"You pass," he stated, with a relieved sigh. "He's a dinger, ain't he?"

"You know 'im, all right." Casey also laughed and put out his hand. "If you're a friend of Kenner's, shake hands with Casey Ryan! He's damned glad to meet yuh—an' you can ask anybody if that ain't the truth."

After that the acquaintance progressed more smoothly. By the time Casey spread his bed close alongside the car—he knew just how much booze Jim Cassidy carried, just what Cassidy expected to make off the load, and a good many other bits of information of no particular use to Casey.

A strange, inner excitement held Casey awake long after Jim Cassidy was asleep snoring. He lay looking up into the leafy branches of the sycamore beside him and watched a star slip slowly across an open space between the branches. Farther up the grove a hilarious group of young hikers sang snatches of songs to the uncertain accompaniment of a ukelele. A hundred feet away on his right, occasional cars went coasting past on the down grade, coming in off the desert, or climbed more slowly with motors working, on their way up from the valley below. The shifting brilliance from their headlights flicked the grove capriciously as they went by. Now and then a car stopped. One, a big, high-powered car with one dazzling spotlight swung into the narrow driveway and entered the grove.

Casey lifted his head like a desert turtle and blinked curiously at the car as it eased past him a few feet and stopped. A gloved hand went out to the spotlight and turned it slowly, lighting the grove foot by foot and pausing to dwell upon each silent, parked car. Casey sat up in the blankets and waited.

Luck, he told himself, was grinning at him from ear to ear. For this was Smiling Lou himself, and none other. He was alone,—a big, hungry, official fish searching the grove greedily. Casey swallowed a grin and tried to look scared. The light was slowly working around in his direction.

I don't suppose Casey Ryan had ever looked really scared in his life. His face simply refused to wear so foreign an expression. Therefore, when the spotlight finally revealed him, Casey blinked against it with a half-hearted grin, as if he had been caught at something foolish. The light remained upon him, and Smiling Lou got out of the car and came back to him slowly.

Not even Casey thought of calling Smiling Lou a fool. He couldn't be and play the game he was playing. Smiling Lou said nothing whatever until he had looked the car over carefully (giving the license number a second sharp glance) and had regarded Casey fixedly while he made up his mind.

"Hullo! Where's your pardner?" he demanded then.

"I'm in pardnerships with myself this trip," Casey retorted. He waited while Smiling Lou looked him over again, more carefully this time.

"Where did you get that car?"

"From Kenner—for sixteen-hundred and seventeen dollars and five cents." Casey fumbled in the blankets—Smiling Lou following his movements suspiciously—and got out the makings of a cigarette.

"Got any booze in that car?" Smiling Lou might have been a traffic cop, for all the trace of humanity there was in his voice.

Casey cocked an eye up at him, sent a quick glance toward the Ford, and looked back into Smiling Lou's face. He hunched his shoulders and finished the making of his cigarette.

"I wisht you wouldn't look," he said glumly. "I got half my outfit in there an' I hate to have it tore up."

Smiling Lou continued to look at him, seeming slightly puzzled. But indecision was not one of his characteristics, evidently. He stepped up to the car, pulled a flashlight from his pocket and looked in.

Casey was up and into his clothes by the time Smiling Lou had uncovered a box or two. Smiling Lou turned toward him, his lips twitching.

"Lift this stuff out of here and put it in my car," he commanded, elation creeping into his voice in spite of himself. "My Lord! The chances you fellows take! Think a dab of paint is going to cover up a brand burnt into the wood?"

Casey looked startled, glancing down into the car to where Smiling Lou pointed.

"The boards is turned over on all the rest," he muttered confidentially. "I dunno how that darned Canadian Club sign got right side up."

"What all have you got?" Smiling Lou lowered his voice when he asked the question. Casey tried not to grin when he replied. Smiling Lou gasped,

"Well, get it into my car, and make it snappy."

Casey made it as snappy as he could, and kept his face straight until Smiling Lou spoke to him sharply.

"I won't take you in to-night with me. I want that car. You drive it into headquarters first thing in the morning. And don't think you can beat it, either. I'll have the road posted. You can knock a good deal off your sentence if you crank up and come in right after breakfast. And make it an early breakfast, too."

His manner was stern, his voice perfectly official. But Casey, eyeing him grimly, saw distinctly the left eyelid lower and lift again.

"All right—I'm the goat," he surrendered and sat down again on his canvas-covered bed. He did not immediately crawl between the blankets, however, because interesting things were happening over at Jim Cassidy's car.

Casey watched Jim Cassidy go picking his way amongst the tree roots and camp litter, his back straightened under the load of hootch he was carrying to Smiling Lou's car. With Jim Cassidy also, Smiling Lou was crisply official. When the last of the hootch had been transferred, Casey heard Smiling Lou tell Jim Cassidy to drive in to headquarters after breakfast next morning—but he did not see Smiling Lou wink when he said it.

After that, Smiling Lou started his motor and drove slowly up through the grove, halting to scan each car as he passed. He swung out through the upper driveway, turned sharply there and came back down the highway speeding up on the downhill grade to San Bernardino.

Jim Cassidy came furtively over and settle down for a whispered conference on Casey's bed.

"How much did he get off'n YOU?" he asked inquisitively. "Did he clean yuh out?"

"Clean as a last year's bone in a kioty den," Casey declared, hiding his satisfaction as best he could. "Never got my roll though."

"He wouldn't—not with you workin' on the inside. Guess it must be kinda touchy around here right now. New officers, mebby. He wouldn't a' cleaned us out if we'd a' been safe. He never came into camp before—not when I've been here. Made that same play to you, didn't he—about givin' yourself up in the morning? Uh course yuh know what that means—DON'T!"

"He shore is foxy, all right," Casey commented with absolute sincerity. "You can ask anybody if he didn't pull it off like the pleasure was all his'n. No L. A. traffic cop ever pinched me an I looked like he enjoyed it more."

"Oh, Lou's cute, all right. They don't any of 'em put anything over on Lou. You must be new at the business, ain't yuh?"

"Second trip," Casey informed him with an air of importance—which he really felt, by the way. "What Casey's studyin' on now, is the next move. No use hangin' around here empty. What do YOU figger on doin'?"

"Well, Lou didn't give no tip—not to me, anyway. So I guess it'll be safe to drive on in to the city and load up again. I got a feller with me—he caught a ride in to San Berdoo; left just before you drove in. Know where to go in the city? 'Cause I can ride in with you, an' let him foller."

"That'll suit me fine," Casey declared. And so they left it for the time being, and Cassidy went back to bed.

A great load had dropped from Casey's shoulders, and he was asleep before Jim Cassidy had ceased to turn restlessly in his blankets. Getting the White Mule out of his car and into the car of Smiling Lou had been the task which Nolan had set for him. What was to happen thereafter Casey could only guess, for Nolan had not told him. And such was the Casey Ryan nature that he made no attempt to solve the problems which Mack Nolan had calmly reserved for himself.

He did not dream, for instance, that Mack Nolan had watched him load the stuff into Smiling Lou's car. He did know that an unobtrusive Cadillac roadster was parked at the next campfire. It had come in half an hour behind him, but the driver had not made any move toward camping until after dark. Casey had glanced his way when the car was parked and the driver got out and began fussing around the car, but he had not been struck with any sense of familiarity in the figure.

There was no reason why he should. Thousands and thousands of men are of Mack Nolan's height and general build. This man looked like a doctor or a dentist perhaps. Beyond the matter of size, similarity to Mack Nolan ceased. The Cadillac man wore a vandyke beard and colored glasses, and a panama and light gray business suit. Casey set him down in his mental catalog as "some town feller" and assumed that they had nothing in common.

Yet Mack Nolan heard nearly every word spoken by Smiling Lou, Casey and Jim Cassidy. (Readers are so inquisitive about these things that I felt I ought to tell you—else you'll be worrying as hard as Casey Ryan did later on. I'm soft-hearted, myself; I never like to worry a reader more than is absolutely necessary. So I'm letting you in, hoping you'll get an added kick out of Casey's further maneuvers).

The Cadillac car, I should explain, was only one of Mack Nolan's little secrets. There is a very good garage at Goffs, not many miles from Juniper Wells. A matter of an hour's driving was sufficient at any time for Mack Nolan to make the exchange. And no man at Goffs would think it very strange that the owner of a Cadillac should prefer to drive a Ford over rough, desert trails to his prospect in the mountains. Mack Nolan, as I have told you before, had a way with him.

CHAPTER TWENTY

With a load of booze in the car and Jim Cassidy by his side, Casey Ryan drove down the long, eucalyptus-shaded avenue that runs past the balloon school at Arcadia and turned into the Foothill Boulevard. Half a mile farther on a Cadillac roadster honked and slid past them, speeding away toward Monrovia. But Casey Ryan was busy talking chummily with Jim Cassidy, and he scarcely knew that a car had passed.

The money he had been given for Smiling Lou had been used to pay for this new load of whisky, and Casey found himself wishing that he could get word of it to Mack Nolan. Still, Nolan's oversight in the matter of arranging for communication between them did not bother Casey much. He was doing his part; if Mack Nolan failed to do his, that was no fault of Casey Ryan's.

At Fontana, where young Kenner had stopped for gas on that eventful first trip of Casey's, Casey slowed down also, for the same purpose, half tempted to call up the Little Woman on long distance while the gas tank was being filled. But presently the matter went clean from his mind—and this was the reason:

A speed cop whose motorcycle stood inconspicuously around the corner of the garage, came forward and eyed the Ford sharply. He drew his little book from his pocket, turned a few leaves, found what he was looking for and eyed again the car. The garage man, slowly turning the crank of the gasoline pump, looked at him inquiringly; but the speed cop ignored the look and turned to Casey.

"Where'd you get this car?" he demanded, in much the same tone which Smiling Lou had used the night before.

"Bought it," Casey told him gruffly.

"Where did you buy it?"

"Over at Goffs, just this side of Needles."

"Got a bill of sale?"

"You got Casey Ryan's word fer it," Casey retorted, with a growing heat inside, where he kept his temper when he wasn't using it.

"Are you Casey Ryan?" The speed cop's eyes hardened just a bit.

"Anybody says I ain't, you send 'em to me—an' then come around in about ten minutes an' look 'em over."

"What's YOUR name?" The officer turned to Jim Cassidy.

"Tom Smith. I was just ketchin' a ride with this feller. Don't go an' mix ME in —I ain't no ways concerned; just ketchin' a ride is all. If I'd 'a' knowed—"

"You can explain that to the judge. Get in there, you, and drive in to San Berdoo. I'll be right with you, so you needn't forget the road!" He stepped back to his motorcycle and pushed it forward.

"Hey! Don't I git paid fer my gas?" the garage man wailed, pulling a dripping nozzle from Casey's gas tank.

"Aw, go tahell!" Casey grunted, and threw a wadded bank note in his direction. "Take that an' shut up. What yuh cryin' around about a gallon uh gas, fer? YOU ain't pinched!"

The money landed near the motorcycle and the officer picked it up, smoothed out the bill, glanced at it and looked through tightened lids at Casey.

"Throwin' money around like a hootch-runner!" he sneered. "I guess you birds need lookn' after, all right. Git goin'!"

Casey "got going." Twice on the way in the officer spurted up alongside and waved him down for speeding. Casey had not intended to speed, either. He was merely keeping pace unconsciously with his thoughts.

He had been told just what he must do if he were arrested for bootlegging, but he was not at all certain that his instructions would cover an arrest for stealing an automobile. Nolan had forgotten about that, he guessed. But Casey's optimism carried him jauntily to jail in San Bernardino, and while he was secretly a bit uneasy, he was not half so worried as Jim Cassidy appeared to be.

Casey was booked—along with "Tom Smith"—on two charges: theft of one Ford car, motor number so-and-so, serial number this-and-that, model, touring, year, whatever-it-was. And, unlawful transportation of spirituous liquor. He tried to give the judge the wink, but without any happy result. So he eventually found himself locked in a cell with Jim Cassidy.

Just at first, Casey Ryan was proud of the part he was playing. He could look with righteous toleration upon the limpness of his fellow prisoner. He could feel secure in the knowledge that he, Casey Ryan, was an agent of the government engaged in helping to uphold the laws of his country.

He waited for an hour or two, listening with a superior kind of patience to Jim Cassidy's panicky unbraidings of his luck. At first Jim was inclined to blame Casey rather bitterly for the plight he was in. But Casey soon stopped that. Young Kenner was the responsible party in this mishap, as Casey very soon made plain to Jim.

"Well, I dunno but what you're right. It WAS kind of a dirty trick—workin' a stole car off onto you. Why didn't he pick some sucker on the outside? Don't line up with Kenner, somehow. Well, I guess mebby Smilin' Lou can see us out uh this hole all right—only I don't like that car-stealin' charge. Mebby Kenner an' Lou can straighten it up, though."

Casey wondered if they could. He wondered, too, how Nolan was going to find out about Smiling Lou getting the camouflaged White Mule. Nolan had not explained that to Casey—but Casey was not worrying yet. His faith in Mack Nolan was firm.

Came bedtime, however, with no sign of official favor toward Casey Ryan. Casey began to wonder. But probably, he consoled himself with thinking, they meant to wait until Jim Cassidy was asleep before they turned Casey loose. He lay on the hard bunk and waited hopefully, listening to the stertorous breathing of Jim Cassidy, who had forgotten his troubles in sleep.

CHAPTER TWENTY-ONE

At noon the next day Casey was still waiting—but not hopefully. "Patience on a monument" couldn't have resembled Casey Ryan in any particular whatever. He was mad. By midnight he had begun to wonder if he was not going to be made a goat again. By daylight, he was positive that he was already a goat. By the time the trusty brought his breakfast, Casey was applying to Mack Nolan the identical words and phrases which he had applied to young Kenner when he was the maddest. Don't ask me to tell you what they were.

Jim Cassidy still clung desperately to his faith in Smiling Lou; but Casey's faith hadn't so much as a finger-hold on anything. What kind of a government was it, he asked himself bitterly, that would leave a trusted agent twenty-four hours shut up in a cell with a whining crook like Jim Cassidy? If, he added pessimistically, he were an agent of the government. Casey doubted it. So far as he could see, Casey Ryan wasn't anything but the goat.

His chief desire now was to get out of there as soon as possible so that he could hunt up Mack Nolan and lick the livin' tar wit of him—or worse. He wanted bail and he wanted it immediately. Not a soul bad come near him, save the trusty, in spite of certain mysterious messages which Casey had sent to the office, asking for an interview with the judge or somebody; Casey didn't care who. Locked in a cell, how was he going to do any of the things Nolan had told him to do if he happened to find himself arrested by an honest officer?

When they hauled him before the police judge, Casey hadn't been given the chance to explain anything to anybody. Unless, of course, he wanted to beller out his business before everybody; and that, he told himself fiercely, was not Casey Ryan's idea of the way to keep a secret. Moreover, that damned speed cop was standing right there, just waiting for a chance to wind his fingers in Casey's collar and choke him off if he tried to say a word. And how the hell, Casey would like to know, was a man going to explain himself when he couldn't get a word in edgeways?

So Casey wanted bail. There were just two ways of getting it, and it went against the grain of his pride to take either one. That is why Casey waited until noon before his Irish stubbornness yielded a bit and he decided to wire me to come. He had to slip the wire out by the underground method—meaning the good will of the trusty. It cost Casey ten dollars, but he didn't grudge that.

He spent that afternoon and most of the night mentally calling the trusty a liar and a thief because there was no reply to the message. As a matter of fact, the trusty sent the wire through as quickly as possible and the fault was mine if any one's. I was too busy hurrying to the rescue to think about sending Casey word that I was coming. Casey said afterwards that my thoughtlessness would be cured for life if I were ever locked in jail and waiting for news.

As it happened, I wired the Little Woman that Casey was in jail again, and caught the first train to San "Berdoo"—coming down by way of Barstow. I could save two or three hours that way, I found, so I told the Little Woman to meet me there and bring all the money she could get her hands on. Not knowing just what Casey was in for this time, it seemed well to be prepared for a good, stiff bail. She beat me by several hours, and between us we had ten thousand dollars.

At that it was a fool's errand. Casey was out of jail and gone before either of us arrived. So there we were, holding the bag, as you might say, and our ten thousand dollars' bail money.

"It's no use asking questions, Jack," the Little Woman told me pensively when we had finished our salad in the best cafe in town, and were waiting for the fish. "I've asked questions of every uniform in this town, from the district judge down to the courthouse janitor. Nobody knows a thing. I DID find that Casey was booked yesterday for having a stolen car and a load of booze in his possession, but he isn't in jail—or if he is, they're keeping him down in some dungeon and have thrown away the key. It was hinted in the police court that he was dismissed for want of evidence; but they wouldn't SAY anything, and so there you are!"

We finished our fish in a thoughtful silence. Then, when the waiter had removed the plates, the Little Woman looked at me with a twinkle in her eyes.

"Well-sir, there's something I want to tell you, Jack. I believe Casey has put this town on the run. They can't tell ME! Something's happened, over around the courthouse. A lot of the men I talked with had a scared look in their eyes, and they were nervous when doors opened, and looked around when people came walking along. I don't know what he's been doing—but Casey Ryan's been up to something. You can't tell ME! I know how our laundry boy looks when Casey's home."

"And didn't you get any line at all on his whereabouts?" I asked her. Given three hours the start of me, I knew perfectly well that the Little Woman had found out all there was to know about Casey.

"Well-sir—I've got this to go on," the Little Woman drawled and held a telegram across the table. "You'll notice that was sent from Goffs. It's ten days old, but I've been getting ready ever since it arrived. I've put Babe in a boarding-school, and I leased the apartment house. I kept three dressmakers ruining their eyes with nightwork, Jack, making up some nifty sports clothes. If Casey's bound to stay in the desert—well, I'm his wife—and Casey does kind of like to have me around. You can't tell ME.

"So I've got the twin-six packed with the niftiest camp outfit you ever saw, Jack. I've got a yellow and red beach umbrella, and two reclining chairs, and— well-sir, I'm going to rough it de luxe. I don't expect to keep Casey in hand—I happen to know him. But it's just possible, Jack, that I can keep him in sight!"

Of course I told her—as I've told her often enough before—that she was a brick. I added that I would go along, if she liked; which she did. Not even the Little Woman should ever attempt to drive across the Mojave alone.

We started out as soon as we had finished the meal. A Cadillac roadster came up behind us and honked for clear passing as we swung into the long, straight stretch that leads up the Cajon. The Little Woman peered into the rear vision mirror and pressed the toe of her white pump upon the accelerator.

"There's only one man in the world that can pass ME on the road," the Little Woman drawled, "and he doesn't wear a panama!"

As we snapped around the turns of Cajon Grade, I looked back once or twice. The Cadillac roadster was still following pertinaciously, but it was too far back to honk at us. When we slid down to the Victorville garage and stopped for gas, the Cadillac slid by. The driver in the panama gave us one glance through his colored glasses, but I felt, somehow, that the glance was sufficiently comprehensive to fix us firmly in his memory. I inquired at the garage concerning Casey Ryan, taking it for granted he would be driving a Ford. A man of that description had stopped at the garage for gas that forenoon, the boy told me. About nine o'clock, I learned from further questioning.

"Well-sir, that gives him five hours the start," the Little Woman remarked, as she eased in the clutch and slid around the corner into the highway to Barstow. "But you can't tell me I can't run down a Ford with this car. I know to the last inch what a Jawn Henry is good for. I drove one myself, remember. Now we'll see."

CHAPTER TWENTY-TWO

At Dagget, the big, blue car with a lady driver sounded the warning signal and passed Mack Nolan and the Cadillac roadster. Like Casey Ryan, Nolan is rather proud of his driving, and with sufficient reason. He was already hurrying, not to overhaul Casey, but to arrive soon after him.

Women drivers loved to pass other cars with a sudden spurt of speed, he had found by experience. They were not, however, consistently fast drivers. Mack Nolan was conscious of a slight irritation when the twin-six took the lead. Somewhere ahead—probably in one of the rough, sandy stretches—he would either have to pass that car or lag behind. Your expert driver likes a clear road ahead.

So Mack Nolan drove a bit harder, and succeeded in getting most of the dust kicked up by the big, blue car. He counted on passing before they reached Ludlow, but he could never quite make it. In that ungodly stretch of sand and rocks and chuck-holes that lies between Ludlow and Amboy, Nolan was sure that the woman driver would have to slow down. He swore a little, too, because she would probably slow down just where passing was impossible. They always did.

They went through Amboy like one party, the big, blue car leading by twenty-five yards. It was a long drive for a woman to make; a hard drive to boot. He wondered if the two in the big car ever ate.

Five miles east of Amboy, when a red sunset was darkening to starlight, the blue car, fifty yards in the lead, overhauled a Ford in trouble. In the loose, sandy trail the big car slowed and stopped abreast of the Ford. There was no passing now, unless Mack Nolan wanted to risk smashing his crank-case on a lava rock, millions of which peppered that particular portion of the Mojave Desert. He stopped perforce.

A pair of feet with legs attached to them, protruded from beneath the running board of the Ford. The Little Woman in the big car leaned over the side and studied the feet critically.

"Casey Ryan, are those the best pair of shoes you own?" she drawled at last. "If you wouldn't wear such rundown heels, you know, you wouldn't look so bow-legged. I've told you and TOLD you that your legs aren't so bad when you wear straight heels."

Casey Ryan crawled out and looked up at her grinning sheepishly.

"They was all right when I left home, ma'am," he defended his shoes mildly. "Desert plays hell with shoe leather—you can ask anybody." Then he added, "Hullo, Jack! What you two think you're doin', anyway. Tryin' t' elope?"

"Why, hello, Ryan!" Mack Nolan greeted, coming up from the Cadillac. "Having trouble with your car?" Casey whirled and eyed Nolan dubiously.

"Naw. This ain't no trouble," he granted. "I only been here four hours or so—this is pastime!"

There was an awkward silence. We in the blue car wanted to know (not at that time knowing) who was the man in the Cadillac roadster, and how he happened to know Casey so well. Nolan, no doubt, wanted to know who we were. And there was so much that Casey wanted to know and needed to know that he couldn't seem to think of anything. However, Casey was the hardest to down. He came up to the side of the blue car, reached in with his hands all greasy black, and took the Little Woman's hand from the wheel and kissed it. The Little Woman made a caressing sound and leaned out to him—and Nolan and I felt that we mustn't look. So our eyes met.

He came around to my side of the car and put out his hand.

"I'm pretty good at guessing," he smiled. "I guess you're Jack Gleason. Casey has talked of you to me. I'm right glad to meet you, too. My name is Mack Nolan, and I'm Irish. I'm Casey Ryan's partner. We have a good—prospect."

Casey looked past the Little Woman and me, straight into Mack Nolan's eyes. I felt something of an electric quality in the air while their gaze held.

"I'm just getting back from a trip down in the valley," Nolan observed easily. "You never did see me in town duds, did you, Casey?" His eyes went to the Little Woman's face and then to me. "I suppose you know what this wild Irishman has just pulled off back there," he said, tilting his head toward San Bernardino, many a mile away to the southwest. "You wouldn't think it to look at him, but he surely has thrown a monkey wrench into as pretty a bootlegging machine as there is in the country. It's such confidential stuff, of course, that you may call it absolutely secret. But for once I'm telling the truth about it.

"Your husband, Mrs. Casey Ryan, holds a commission from headquarters as a prohibition officer. A deputy, it is true,—but commissioned nevertheless. He's just getting back from a very pretty piece of work. A crooked officer named Smiling Lou was arrested last night. He had all kinds of liquor cached away in his house. Casey can tell you sometime how he trapped him.

"Of course, I'm just an amateur mining expert on a vacation, myself." His eyes met Casey's straight. "I wasn't with him when he pulled the deal, but I heard about it afterwards, and I knew he was planning something of the sort when he left camp. How I happened to know about the commission," he added, reaching into his pocket, "is because he left it with me for safe keeping. I'm going to let you look at it—just in case he's too proud to let it out of his hands once I give it back.

"Now, of course, I'm talking like an old woman and telling all Casey's secrets —and you'll probably see a real Irish fight when he gets in reach of me. But I knew he hadn't told you exactly what he's doing, and—I personally feel that his wife and his best friend are entitled to know as much as his partner knows about him."

The Little Woman nodded absently her thanks. She was holding Casey's commission under the dash-light to read it.

I saw Casey gulp once or twice while he stared across the car at Mack Nolan. He pushed his dusty, black hat forward over one eyebrow and reached into his pocket.

"Aw, hell," he grunted, grinning queerly. "You come around here oncet, Mr. Nolan, where I can git my hands on yuh!"

Nevada
hates city, married
IRISH
moonshine

Printed in the USA
CPSIA information can be obtained
at www.ICGtesting.com
LVHW071958141223
766562LV00012B/886

9 781517 117764